DATE:

_____

TO:

_____

FROM:

_____

Made to Shine: 90 Devotions to Enjoy and Reflect God's Light
Copyright © 2020 April Rodgers. All Rights Reserved.
First Edition, May 2020

Published by:

DaySpring

21154 Highway 16 East
Siloam Springs, AR 72761
dayspring.com

Written by April Rodgers
Cover Design and Typeset by Greg Jackson of thinkpen.design

Printed in China
Prime: J2098
ISBN: 978-1-64454-657-4

MADE
TO
SHINE

90 Devotions to Enjoy and

Reflect God's Light

APRIL RODGERS

DaySpring

TABLE OF CONTENTS

MADE TO SHINE

You were made to shine!

Jesus said to live so that when others see your light and the good works that you do, they will praise your Father in heaven (Matthew 5:16). That's a really big deal. If we live out our calling to SHINE, then the God of all creation gets the praise that He is due. Once we realize our purpose in this life, then we can live with intentionality in our everyday lives, allowing everything that we do to reflect the light that was put inside of us by Jesus Himself.

Within every geographical location as well as every generation there exist divine opportunities to point others to God. Just as the beautiful and young Queen Esther was told by her wise uncle when she was faced with a life-or-death situation,

> Who knows, perhaps you have come to your royal position for such a time as this (Esther 4:14 CSB).

Esther did not run from the situation but instead rose to the challenge and was able to shine.

Just as Esther shone, you too, my friend, have been appointed for such a time as this to shine right where you are by taking your everyday life activities and using them as an opportunity to point others to Christ.

In the workplace, in the classroom, in the car pickup line, in the gym, in the restaurant, and in our homes, we are called to let our lights shine in all of these places so that others are attracted to the only thing that matters: a relationship with the one true God.

Let's be women who resolve to rise to the challenge and let our lights shine. Who knows, perhaps you were made to shine for such a time as this!

LORD, STRENGTHEN US TO BE WOMEN WHO ARE
WILLING TO SHINE FOR YOU IN EVERY ASPECT
OF OUR LIVES SO THAT YOU ARE PRAISED!

FELLOWSHIP IN THE LIGHT

Few things bind our hearts together like sharing a meal together. It never fails that when we take the time to sit down and break bread, the conversation starts flowing. However, in our fast-paced world of texting, where full conversations can be had via emojis, true fellowship can be hard to come by.

I John 1:7 (NIV) states,

> *If we walk in the light, as He is in the light, we have fellowship with one other, and the blood of Jesus, His Son, purifies us from all sin.*

One of the definitions of fellowship is "to share, or a close mutual association." This is important because God intended us to share our lives together so that we can encourage each other to live in the light. If we are Christ followers, then hopefully our relationship with Jesus will work itself into the conversation, and if we aren't, then what better way to be introduced to the best thing that ever happened—Jesus' life-giving sacrifice—while sharing life together around the table?

The point is simply to intentionally share your life and your light with others. Who is it that you could invite over for a meal or ask to lunch this week?

There may be someone at the table who still needs to hear about how the blood of Jesus can cleanse us from all sin. Or it could be that the Lord simply wants you to encourage your family members or friends in their walk with Christ. It's possible that you're interested in Jesus and you'd like to know more about Him. Whatever your situation, open your life up to others and be willing to fellowship in the LIGHT!

LORD, WE ASK THAT YOU PROVIDE US WITH
DIVINE OPPORTUNITIES TO SHARE OUR LIVES WITH
OTHERS AS WE STRIVE TO LIVE IN YOUR LIGHT.

ABIDE

She breathed in deeply the sweetest of all scents, the smell of newborn baby. It had been years since she'd had a baby of her own so she jumped at every chance to hold her new nephew.

After she fed him his bottle, he immediately went to sleep in her arms, his soft breathing lulling her into a state of rest. She thought of all the work that needed to be done but decided it could wait. This was more important. With each soft snore that he made, her soul became more and more still. As she soaked in the moment, it reminded her of what it means to truly abide.

Jesus said in John 15:9 (NASB),

> *Just as the Father has loved Me,*
> *I have also loved you; abide in My love.*

The word *abide* in the original language also carries these definitions: "to remain, to dwell," and my personal favorite, "to be held."

The practice of abiding was so important to Jesus because He knew that it was the life-giving source of all activity. In fact, if we are not abiding in Him, we can do nothing (John 15:5). Our connection to Him is vital for our growth as Christ followers, but it also gives us the capacity to feel loved by Him.

One of the ways that we abide is by taking time daily to spend with the Lord. As we read His Word and pray to Him, we feel that love inside us growing stronger with each passing day. Jesus loves each one of us so fully and completely.

Just as the newborn baby was content to be held and loved, allow yourself to feel the love of your Savior. Just abide.

JESUS, HELP US TO FIND A MOMENT TODAY TO REST IN YOUR PRESENCE. WE KNOW THAT IT'S IN THOSE QUIET MOMENTS THAT WE FEEL YOUR LOVE SURROUND US AS WE SIMPLY ABIDE IN YOU.

ALWAYS PRAISE

She excitedly slid into the chair opposite her mentor at the coffee shop and immediately began telling him of how God had answered a prayer that she had been praying for many years.

When she finally took a breath, the wise mentor looked at her with kind eyes and said, "That's wonderful news. However, did you take the time to praise God for answering you? The appropriate response is always praise."

Hmmm, had she? It was certainly evident that she was thankful. Yet after she gave it some thought, she realized that she hadn't stopped long enough to offer her praise back to the One who had answered her long-awaited prayer.

In Luke 18:43 (NIV), after Jesus healed the blind beggar, the Bible says,

> *Immediately he received his sight and*
> *followed Jesus, praising God. When all the*
> *people saw it, they also praised God.*

Can you just imagine this scene from years ago? A Hallelujah Praise Party was going on in the streets of Jericho all because of what Jesus did for one man.

We have to be willing to do the same in our own lives. When God answers that prayer that you've been bringing to Him for some time now, take the time to praise Him. And when you do, others will undoubtedly follow your lead, because who can resist a good praise party?

The appropriate response to answered prayer is always praise!

JESUS, WE LIFT UP OUR PRAISE TO YOU TODAY JUST LIKE THE PEOPLE OF JERICHO DID WHEN YOU HEALED THE BLIND BEGGAR. HELP US TO STOP AND REMEMBER THAT OUR FIRST RESPONSE TO ANSWERED PRAYER IS TO PRAISE YOU, AND THEN TO TELL THE WORLD OF YOUR GOODNESS.

BE A BLESSING

Ever since her children were young, anytime she dropped them off at school or at a friend's house, she would hug them tight and tell them to "be a blessing." Sometimes the little darlings would heed such sound advice and do as they were told, and other times they could use some improvement, but nevertheless, they were sent out into the world each day with the admonishment to be a blessing to their teachers and friends.

What exactly does it mean to be a blessing?

Jesus reminds us in Luke 6:45 (The Message),

> *It's who you are, not what you say and*
> *do, that counts. Your true being brims*
> *over into true words and deeds.*

Out of the overflow of our hearts, we become a blessing.

Being a blessing is as easy as paying for the coffee of the person behind you in the car line and leaving them a little note that says you are praying that their day is filled with light.

Or perhaps you pay a quick visit to a sleep-deprived mom who has been stuck indoors caring for her newborn. Can't you just imagine her thankfulness for an hour of adult conversation?

Being a blessing doesn't have to be elaborate or time-consuming. It's simply finding ways to let your true self brim over into every aspect of your life…in your social media comments, in traffic leaving the church parking lot, in the words that you exchange with your spouse, and even in the quiet moments when you think no one is watching.

The beautiful thing about being a blessing is that people respond to the light that you are giving off. They may not even realize that you are pointing them straight to Jesus. What better reason to be a blessing!

LORD, GIVE US OPPORTUNITIES TO BE A
BLESSING TO THOSE WE COME INTO CONTACT
WITH TODAY. LET US REFLECT YOUR LIGHT
IN BOTH OUR WORDS AND DEEDS.

HARVEST WORKERS

A pecan orchard sat adjacent to a neighborhood school. The owner of the orchard had told the children of the school that if they found a pecan on the ground, they were welcome to keep it.

One little boy took this invitation to heart and saw it as a challenge to find as many pecans as he possibly could during recess, filling his pockets to the brim.

It gave the generous land owner much pleasure to watch the children gather the excess nuts, knowing that each one was a prize to the child who took the time to find it among the dried leaves and dirt. He had even installed a pecan-cracking station so that they could open up the shells and retrieve the delicious nuts on the spot.

Jesus speaks of a harvest in Matthew 9:37–38 (NIV) when He tells His disciples,

The harvest is plentiful, but the workers are few. Ask the Lord of the harvest, therefore, to send out workers into His harvest field.

God wants more than anything for all of His children to have eternal life, and He needs workers who are willing to point others to Jesus Christ as their Lord and Savior.

However, this requires diligence to look beyond the surface to find those prized souls.

Just as the boy was willing to get his hands dirty in order to find the pecans, we should be willing to be a harvest worker for the Lord. The results are eternal and the hard work is worth it!

Accept the challenge and ask the Lord of the harvest to send you out today.

LORD OF THE HARVEST, WE ASK THAT YOU
SEND US OUT TO DO YOUR KINGDOM WORK.
WE HUMBLY ACCEPT THE CHALLENGE AND
ARE WILLING TO DO THE HARD WORK IT
TAKES TO BRING OTHERS TO YOUR LIGHT.

UNCERTAIN TIMES

We live in a world filled with uncertainty.

It seems as if every time we turn on the news there's another disaster or death by shooting. It can be scary and daunting. Our hearts break for the victims and their families, and we become keenly aware that evil exists in the world. It can make us want to build bubbles around ourselves and our families, and before long we find that we are living in a state of paranoia.

But God never called us to live a life of fear or to bury our heads in the sand. He said that we are to take refuge in Him and be glad even in the midst of uncertainty.

King David prayed to the Lord in Psalm 5:11 (NIV),

But let all who take refuge in You be glad; let them ever sing for joy. Spread Your protection over them, that those who love Your name may rejoice in You.

David knew a thing or two about uncertain times. But he also knew to put his trust in a mighty God, the only One who could provide the protection he desperately needed. David also knew that joy is a choice and those who love the name of the Lord have a reason to rejoice.

David's point in saying this was not to discount the heaviness of the situation he was facing, and we shouldn't either. Yet we do get to make the choice of how we are going to operate in our everyday lives.

We can't control the weather or gunmen who take the lives of the innocent, but we can pray. The question is, are we going to choose fear over faith? Or are we going to choose JOY and ask for protection from the One who can provide it? Even through the tears we can sing for joy, placing our faith in a mighty God.

JESUS, COME AND WRAP YOUR ARMS AROUND THE BROKENHEARTED. WE DON'T UNDERSTAND SUCH SENSELESS TRAGEDY, BUT WE DON'T GIVE IN TO FEAR EITHER. WE TAKE REFUGE IN YOU AND ASK THAT YOU SPREAD YOUR PROTECTION OVER US AND OUR FAMILIES. WE REJOICE IN YOU ALONE.

LIGHT FOR LITTLE CHILDREN

Her daughter had consistently been making the same comment for weeks now: "Mommy, I'm ready to let Jesus come into my heart." But every time the little girl said it, the mom told her she was too young to make such an important decision.

But God in His perfect timing knew His little child should not be hindered to come to Him, so He allowed the little girl's godly babysitter to hear her heart. The babysitter asked why the girl was waiting, to which she responded, "My mom doesn't think I'm ready." The babysitter probed a little more and then prayed with her on the spot to receive her salvation.

Later that night the little girl ran to greet her mother and exclaimed, "I let Jesus come into my heart tonight!" And her motherly instinct told her that it was indeed the right timing. They rejoiced with the angels that night with a joyful celebration.

In Luke 18:16–17 (HCSB), Jesus has specific instructions on how to handle situations such as these,

Let the little children come to Me, and don't stop them, because the kingdom of God belongs to such as these. I assure you: Whoever does not welcome the kingdom of God like a little child will never enter it.

As adults we often overthink these situations, wondering if a child is truly able to grasp the magnitude of what Jesus has done for them on the cross. But the bigger question is: can anybody fully understand this amazing grace?

No, and that is why it is easier for a child to enter God's kingdom, because all it takes is simple faith to grab hold of the light.

JESUS, THANK YOU FOR YOUR LESSON ON
HOW TO LET THE LITTLE CHILDREN COME INTO
YOUR LIGHT. REMOVE US WHEN NECESSARY
SO THAT WE DON'T HINDER THEM FROM
COMING TO YOU. ALSO, KEEP US SEEKING
YOUR KINGDOM WITH A CHILDLIKE FAITH.

IN LIGHT OF SUCCESS

Zig Ziglar once said, "You were designed for accomplishment, engineered for success, and endowed with the seeds of greatness." Yet in order to achieve these three things—accomplishment, success, and greatness—it is imperative that we have a good plan in place. Planning may or may not come naturally to you; however, it is essential in light of success.

But did you know that having a good plan in place is not the most important thing that we can do in order to achieve greatness? It is only a part of the process.

Proverbs 16:9 (NLT) says,

> *We can make our plans, but the*
> *LORD determines our steps.*

If we are diligent to plan, then we can better manage expectations and react smartly when that inevitable curveball is thrown our way. We simply cannot and should not expect to control everything in our lives. Sometimes life just happens. Step by step we need to trust God with everything in our lives. That includes our marriages, our kids, our finances, and our dreams. Is this always easy? No, certainly not. But the end result is worth it!

Proverbs 16:3 tells us,

Commit your actions to the LORD,
and your plans will succeed.

So, make your plans and work hard to stay on track, but also take the time to commit those plans to the Lord because His promise to make you successful in your planning is something that you do not want to miss out on. After all, He's the only one with a 100 percent success rate!

GOD, WE COMMIT OUR ACTIONS TO YOU TODAY. WE
ASK THAT YOU DIRECT OUR STEPS AS WE STRIVE
TO PUT A GOOD PLAN IN PLACE, BUT HELP US TO
ALSO TRUST YOU TO WORK OUT THE DETAILS.
OUR SENSE OF ACCOMPLISHMENT, SUCCESS, AND
GREATNESS ARE COMPLETELY IN YOUR HANDS.

A SPIRIT OF GENTLENESS

She couldn't quite put her finger on it, but something was off at home.

The kids were constantly bickering with each other. She often found that she and her husband were short with their words. No one was being outright rude, but no one was being gentle either. And her spirit had had enough.

It was then she realized that a change first needed to happen in her heart. She instantly prayed out loud, "Lord, help me change this spirit of dissension in my home." She opened up her Bible to the book of Philippians, where it seems there were two women in the church who were not getting along so well.

Paul gave these words of advice to them when he said in Philippians 4:5 (NIV),

Let your gentleness be evident to all. The Lord is near.

The change must first start with us. If we ourselves are not first exhibiting gentleness to our loved ones, how can we expect them to be gentle with each other? But if we are willing to reflect a spirit of gentleness in our speech and actions, we will typically begin to see a positive change in them as well.

However, our ultimate motivation for treating our families with gentleness is that we believe that the Lord is near and we want to reflect the spirit of gentleness that He gives to us. God is consistently gentle with us, never speaking in a harsh tone but gently leading us to repentance.

We may not get it right 100 percent of the time, but if we are willing to be led by the Spirit, then gentleness will be sure to follow.

LORD, HELP US TO REMEMBER PAUL'S WORDS
AND LET OUR GENTLENESS BE EVIDENT TO EVERY
SINGLE PERSON WE INTERACT WITH, REFLECTING
THE VERY SAME SPIRIT OF GENTLENESS THAT
YOU POSSESS. THANK YOU FOR BEING NEAR
AND INSTRUCTING US IN HOW TO SHINE WITH
A GENTLE SPIRIT IN OUR EVERYDAY LIVES.

WE ARE TOLD TO LET
OUR LIGHT SHINE, AND
IF IT DOES, WE WON'T
NEED TO TELL ANYBODY
IT DOES. LIGHTHOUSES
DON'T FIRE CANNONS
TO CALL ATTENTION
TO THEIR SHINING—
THEY JUST SHINE.

Dwight L. Moody

COMMIT TO HIS WAY

There is an old camel in Israel on the Mount of Olives that gives countless rides to enthusiastic tourists every day.

One might expect a camel to deliver a relatively smooth ride; however, this was not the experience for a group of middle-aged tourists. This particular camel did not seem pleased that he had to kneel down once again just to get another eager rider on his back. The riders hung on for dear life as they took a quick trip around the path, and they were thankful that the camel didn't spit on them as he knelt back down to roll them off. He obviously was not enjoying his work.

David instructs us in Psalm 37:5–6 (HCSB),

> *Commit your way to the LORD;*
> *trust in Him, and He will act, making*
> *your righteousness shine like the dawn.*

What's surprising is that the word *commit* means "to roll away," as in the way a camel kneels down and allows the load it's carrying to roll off.

When we commit our works to the Lord we allow the load of work, deadlines, ministry, motherhood, or what- ever it is that is weighing us down to roll into the hands of the Lord. And what capable hands they are! They created us after all.

What's even better is that once we allow all that weight to roll off of us, it frees us to "shine like the dawn." Trusting in His way is a sure way to shine in our everyday lives!

If today you feel the pressure to carry around that work load all by yourself, remember to kneel down before your Lord and let it roll off of you. But maybe with a little more finesse than that old camel in Israel.

GOD, WE KNEEL BEFORE YOU TODAY TO RELEASE THE
WEIGHT THAT WE HAVE BEEN CARRYING AROUND
UNNECESSARILY. WE TRUST YOU TO ACT ON OUR
BEHALF AND TO MAKE US SHINE LIKE THE DAWN.

FATHER OF LIGHTS

When she was a little girl the shadows that danced on her wall at night seemed larger than life. She knew that the shadows couldn't hurt her, but that didn't stop her from crying out for her mother when they shifted on the wall. Her mother would come into her room and reassure her that they were simply spots of darkness, but to the little girl they were always moving around and they couldn't be trusted. The only thing that could make her feel better was to turn the lights on and, wouldn't you know it, the shadows would immediately disappear in the presence of LIGHT.

James 1:17 (NIV) tells us,

> *Every good and perfect gift is from above, coming down from the Father of the heavenly lights, who does not change like shifting shadows.*

Wow! What a Father we have! He gives us good and perfect gifts. Gifts of strength and salvation. But not only that, He also gives us the gift of security. He knows that this world can be dark and scary, with shadows shifting before our very eyes. But we don't have to be afraid, because our Father is a father of lights and His presence immediately dispels the darkness.

How wonderful it is to know that He doesn't change. He could never be a shadow dancing on the wall that can't be trusted. Because He is truth and He is LIGHT!

WHAT A GOOD FATHER YOU ARE! THANK YOU FOR BRINGING LIGHT INTO OUR LIVES AND FOR DISPELLING THE DARKNESS WITH YOUR AWESOME PRESENCE. LET US BE AWARE OF YOUR GOOD AND PERFECT GIFTS.

INSIDE OUT

She was feeling a little blah while routinely applying her same old makeup and said to her reflection in the mirror, "I could really use a makeover."

She grabbed her purse and her keys and headed out the door to her favorite department store. The woman at the beauty counter did a wonderful job of applying a little bit of blush here and a touch of lip gloss there. When she finally snuck a peek at her reflection, she was truly impressed with what she saw in the mirror. But as pretty as it made her feel in the moment, she knew that the results were only temporary.

She needed something more lasting. She needed a change from the inside out.

When John the Baptist was baptizing Jesus in the Jordan River, he said this,

> [Jesus'] baptism—a holy baptism by the
> Holy Spirit—will change you from the
> inside out (Mark 1:8 The Message).

How revolutionary to know that we already have the Holy Spirit living inside of us and therefore have access to everything that we need to live a fulfilled life. We just have to allow Him to transform us into changed women.

We need to sit down at God's counter and apply the foundation of His Word first. Then we add in prayer in order to see the reflection that we desire.

It's a daily discipline that only the Holy Spirit can help us achieve. Yes, there will be days when we fail to get it right. But how wonderful it will be when we get to heaven and Jesus holds up a mirror for us to look in. The reflection will be absolutely stunning because it bears His face.

HOLY SPIRIT, COME AND TRANSFORM US INTO WOMEN WHO SHINE FOR YOU. LET US BE WILLING TO WORK ON OUR REFLECTION BY READING YOUR WORD AND PRAYING DAILY.

MOVING ON

It's always a little awkward to walk into a crowd where you don't know anyone. It's even more awkward if no one breaks off from their circle to welcome you or at the very least simply acknowledge that you're in the room. This is when smartphones become extremely handy because at the very least you can give off the impression that someone somewhere desires your attention.

Jesus knew what it felt like to be an outcast. He was constantly facing opposition because of the gospel message that He was teaching, and He even warned the disciples that this would happen to them as well. In Luke 9:5 (The Message) He gives them these specific instructions:

If you're not welcomed, leave town. Don't make a scene. Shrug your shoulders and move on.

If we have decided to live gospel-centered lives, then we will not always be welcome in every social setting. In fact, Scripture lets us know that not everyone is living in the light, and as we shine they may be uncomfortable because the darkness is exposed by the light. There will undoubtedly be those awkward moments in which we'll have to resolve to recognize in advance when it's time to politely leave the party. This won't always be easy, but it will be worth it in the end.

So, if you find yourself in one of these awkward situations, don't take it personally. Instead, take Jesus' advice: gather your belongings and move on down the road. There's someone somewhere who needs to hear some Good News and they'll welcome you to join their circle.

JESUS, WE WANT TO SHINE FOR YOU BUT WE KNOW THAT THERE WILL BE TIMES WE'LL BE IN PLACES WHERE THE GOSPEL IS NOT WELCOME. HELP US TO KNOW WHEN IT'S TIME TO STAY AND WHEN IT'S TIME TO MOVE ON DOWN THE ROAD.

FOLLOW MY EXAMPLE

Few things will make a mother sit up straight and pay attention like knowing that little eyes are watching her.

She had visited the nail salon to get a French manicure for an upcoming event. She rarely got her nails painted and was pleased with the classy finish they provided.

The event came, and while she was away her youngest daughter went to her grandmother's house to play. When the mother came home, the little girl burst through the door and shouted, "Mama, look! I have white tips too!"

Normally this particular child would have asked for the brightest, sparkliest nail color on the market because that's just how she rolled, but that day she chose to follow her mother's example.

The mother hugged her precious child tightly and told her how beautiful those white-tipped nails looked, while inwardly she was hit with the gravity of what had just happened. She thanked God for the valuable lesson on how she must pay close attention to the things she followed because that determined what and, more importantly, who her child followed.

The apostle Paul took his job of providing a good example very seriously. He told the church in Corinth,

Follow my example, as I follow the example
of Christ (I Corinthians 11:1 NIV).

Because Paul was following the best example possible, he had full confidence that he could instruct others to follow him. That doesn't mean that Paul didn't stumble from time to time. It just means that because he was following closely after Christ, he was able to make more right decisions than wrong.

Whether we are mothers or not, there are impressionable people within our circles of influence who are watching our examples. As women of light, we are given the serious yet spectacular privilege of leading others straight to Christ. All we have to do is keep our eyes on Jesus and follow His example.

JESUS, FIX OUR EYES ON YOUR EXAMPLE. IT
MATTERS BECAUSE OTHER EYES ARE WATCHING
AND IT MATTERS BECAUSE YOUR EYES ARE TOO.

POINTING OTHERS TO CHRIST

Billy Graham once said, "When Christ hung, and bled, and died on the cross, it was God saying to the world, 'I love you.'"

Regarded as one of the world's greatest preachers, Billy Graham lived to be ninety-nine years old. The impact that this one man had on the world for the gospel is too great to quantify.

Numerous stories have surfaced over the years of how Billy Graham's preaching has changed the lives of many and led them to a relationship with Jesus Christ. One such story includes that of Louis Zamperini, the man who inspired the book *Unbroken* by Lauren Hillenbrand. Louis was held as a prisoner of war in a Japanese camp and was brutally abused by an officer nicknamed The Bird. After Louis's release from the POW camp he returned to the United States, but as one can imagine, he lived with hatred for his oppressor. One evening he heard Billy Graham preach and he gave his life to Christ on the spot. That bold decision gave him the courage to offer The Bird supernatural forgiveness.

How many other stories are out there because of Billy Graham's persistence to preach the gospel? He never gave up spreading the Good News, and because of his faithfulness, countless men and women came to know God's message of love and forgiveness.

Psalm 105:1 (NIV) tells us,

Give praise to the Lord, proclaim His name; make known among the nations what He has done.

We too are presented with opportunities to share the Good News in our everyday lives, telling of a God who loves so extravagantly that His Son hung, bled, and died on a cross. We may never be world-renowned preachers, but we can do what we can, where we can to point others to Christ, reminding the world that God loves them.

LORD, HELP US TO BE BOLD TO LET OUR LIGHTS SHINE FOR YOU JUST AS BILLY GRAHAM DID. WE WANT TO POINT OTHERS TO YOU SO THAT THEY CAN HEAR YOUR MESSAGE OF LOVE AND FORGIVENESS.

SERVING UP YOUR GIFT

She had planned for this day for months, and it was finally here. The Mother's Day brunch looked beautiful, with gorgeous floral arrangements and colorful tablecloths. The stage was set for the speakers and the volunteers were in their places with welcoming smiles on their beautiful faces.

And while she was so glad it had all come together, she knew that the event wasn't successful because of her but because of all the people who helped—all the people who used their various gifts to serve the Lord.

In I Peter 4:10 (NIV) we read,

Each of you should use whatever gift you have received to serve others, as faithful stewards of God's grace in its various forms.

Peter is simply stating that we all have our own unique gifts and we should use them to serve others. When we do this, God's grace is poured out in different ways onto those we serve, making for a desirable overall experience.

But here's where the trap comes into play. Sometimes we start comparing our gift to our sister's gift and we believe the enemy's lies when he tells us, "Your gift isn't special. It's not nearly as good as hers is. You don't have anything to offer so you might as well stay home." Don't believe that for a single second! Without you faithfully administering YOUR gift, the blessing for those present will never be as great as it could be.

It takes all the gifts to have a successful day of worship! Whether it be leading, singing, painting, speaking, or cooking, your gift is both unique and needed.

You are essential to the successful administration of God's grace. Without you, it just won't be as special. So, serve up your gift!

FATHER, WE LOOK TO YOU FOR GUIDANCE ON
HOW TO SERVE WITH OUR UNIQUE GIFT THAT
YOU HAVE GIVEN US. LET US RESIST THE VOICE
OF THE ENEMY AND BE WILLING TO ADMINISTER
YOUR AMAZING GRACE TO THOSE WE SERVE.

JUST BREATHE

If you can, close your eyes and take a moment to just breathe. Feel your breath start to move in and out, and as you do, start to visualize yourself breathing in the Holy Spirit and breathing out your anxiety. Spirit in. Anxiety out.

Worry is such a natural part of our everyday lives. We worry about what we're going to eat, wear, drive, achieve. What will our kids grow up to be? How will we afford that house? What if we get sick? Will people judge us if we let our light shine? Before long we're all knotted up and popping antacids like there's no tomorrow.

But what if instead of worrying about things beyond our control, we put the responsibility on the One who actually does have the power to control such things?

I Peter 5:7 NIV says,

Cast all your anxiety on Him because He cares for you.

The verb *cast* means to "stop worrying and trust," but it also means to "put responsibility on" another. Peter is telling us that we can put all the responsibility on God to take care of those worries for us. Additionally, the word *all* means exactly that: ALL…every. single.one. No concern is too small or too large for our great God. He takes responsibility for each one, and His reasoning is simply that He wants to. His concern is for us! He cares so much about every detail of our lives that He was willing to do what no one else would even consider. That's a whole lot of care, friend!

So, the next time anxiety creeps back into our thoughts, we remember how deeply He cares and we put the responsibility on the One who can carry the load. Breathe in His Spirit. Exhale out the anxiety. Just breathe.

HOLY SPIRIT, COME AND HELP US TO RELEASE THIS
LOAD OF RESPONSIBILITY TO YOU. WE BELIEVE
YOU WHEN YOU SAY THAT YOU CARE FOR US,
AND WE BREATHE IN YOUR PRESENCE NOW.

THE PEOPLE WALKING IN DARKNESS
HAVE SEEN A GREAT LIGHT;
ON THOSE LIVING IN THE LAND OF
DEEP DARKNESS
A LIGHT HAS DAWNED.

ISAIAH 9:2 NIV

ONLY A BREATH

There's nothing more refreshing than seeing trees start to bud in the spring, especially after a long, cold winter. Typically, the Japanese magnolia tree is the first to bud, with its tulip-like flowers, ranging from white-pink to deep purple. They are a reminder that spring is on the way, despite the volatile weather. And if the weather does cooperate, then usually they will last for up to four weeks, adding splashes of color that brightly stand out against the brown dormant grass and shrubs. However, if a late frost blows through, the petals can be damaged and they won't reach their full potential.

These trees provide subtle reminders of the frailty and brevity of life, but they also reveal the beauty of it.

We never know when an unexpected frost is going to blow through and shorten a bud's life, robbing it of its full life span. If you have ever lost a loved one who died unexpectedly at a young age, then you understand the chilling pain this involves.

But on the flip side, a person may live a long and full life yet never meet their maximum potential. Fear of the elements may stunt their growth and they never bloom with the beauty that God intended them to.

Psalm 39:5 (NCV) reminds us of how fleeting this life is for each of us,

Everyone's life is only a breath.

That Scripture isn't meant to discourage us, but rather to encourage us to be intentional with the days that God has given us. Yes, life is short, but those who are always reaching toward the light are the ones who produce the most beautiful of flowers.

LORD, WE DON'T KNOW HOW LONG OUR LIFE ON THIS EARTH WILL BE; THAT'S ENTIRELY UP TO YOU. BUT WE CAN BE INTENTIONAL WITH THE WAY THAT WE CHOOSE TO LIVE. ENCOURAGE US TO KEEP REACHING TOWARD THE LIGHT EACH AND EVERY DAY.

MUCH TO DISCUSS

She sat across from her mentor at their favorite Mexican restaurant, not realizing that it would be their last time together on this side of eternity. She knew that her mentor had not been feeling well and gave her the option to reschedule their lunch, but the generous mentor wouldn't think of it. She assured her friend that she was well enough to meet. "And besides," she said, "there is much to discuss."

And indeed there was much to discuss! Even though she couldn't have known for certain, the mentor spoke as if her time was short, dispensing as much advice as she could in a two-hour time span.

When she received word the next week that her mentor had passed from this life and gone to be with Jesus, her heart was broken, but she also praised God for the time that He had given her with this extraordinary, light-shining woman.

What a blessing it is to have wise mentors who can speak life into us, but we mustn't forget that we have access to the same revelation-light that they do. God beckons us to come and open His Word, whispering to our souls that there is much to discuss. In Psalm 119:130 (TPT), we read,

Break open Your word within me until
revelation-light shines out! Those with open
hearts are given insight into Your plans.

And as we come with open hearts, what we find is that He gives us divine insight into His plans for our lives, downloading as much advice and knowledge as we can handle in a short amount of time.

As we keep coming back day after day and growing in His Word, we may just find ourselves sitting as a wise mentor for another, letting His revelation-light shine out of us. After all, there is much to discuss.

O LORD, LET US BE WOMEN WHO BREAK OPEN
YOUR WORD ON A DAILY BASIS SO THAT WE
CAN BE GIVEN INSIGHT INTO YOUR PLANS FOR
OUR LIVES. WE DESIRE TO BE WOMEN WHO
SHINE WITH YOUR REVELATION-LIGHT!

BAKING COOKIES

As the aroma of fresh chocolate chip cookies filled the home, the preteen girl expectantly watched them bake in the oven. She had come home from school craving the sweet treat, asking her mom if they had any cookie dough on hand.

Her mom replied, "We don't, honey. Why don't you make us some?"

So she did, from start to finish. She diligently followed the recipe, creaming the butter and sugars, carefully adding the eggs one at a time. Mixing in the flour, vanilla, and finally the chocolate chips. And of course, like any good baker, she tasted her work along the way.

As she pulled the warm cookies out of the oven, the girl was proud of herself and her accomplishment. But the real reward was seeing her family enjoy the cookies with tall glasses of cold milk.

Proverbs 12:14 NIV tells us,

*From the fruit of their lips people are
filled with good things, and the work of
their hands brings them reward.*

In this verse we learn two lessons: first, we ought to let the words that we speak be sweet as chocolate chips, and second, we have to actually put in the work if we want to enjoy the cookies.

As women of light, we know that it takes hard work to reap the rewards that we desire. But the true opportunity to shine comes when we allow our words to bring life to others, filling them with good things, leaving the sweet taste on their lips, just like chocolate chip cookies.

LORD, ALLOW THIS PROVERB TO SINK INTO
OUR ACTIONS AS WE STRIVE TO SHINE
YOUR LIGHT, LETTING OUR WORDS BE
SWEET AND OUR WORK BE DILIGENT.

NOT ASHAMED

Imagine your best friend is drowning in the middle of the lake and you are standing on the bank with an inner tube and a rope. But instead of throwing it to her, you try to hide it behind your back sheepishly because you are ashamed that your inner tube may not be what she needs in this moment or that it is inadequate to meet her needs. All the while she's gasping for air, her head dangerously close to going under for good. At this point she doesn't care if your inner tube is pink or in the shape of a unicorn or even deflated a little. She'll take anything you've got, yet still you hold out on her, unwilling to give her the very thing that will save her life.

How absurd would that be? You would never just sit there and watch her drown knowing that you have just what she needs to be rescued. Your instincts would kick in and you would do whatever it took to get your friend to safety.

Jesus recognized the absurdity of hiding our life-giving light when He preached the Sermon on the Mount. He challenged His followers to let their light shine, mentioning how pointless it would be to hide their light under a bowl.

The apostle Paul echoed this message when he said,

I am NOT ashamed of the gospel, because it is the power of God that brings salvation to everyone who believes (Romans 1:16 NIV, emphasis added).

We should not/cannot/will not be ashamed of what Christ has done for us. Especially because we know that it has the power to save others, just as it did for us. If we have had a true, life-changing encounter with Jesus, then there is no reason why we should not be willing to take His light and allow it to shine for others to see.

JESUS, WE ARE NOT ASHAMED OF WHAT YOU HAVE DONE FOR US. THANK YOU FOR YOUR GIFT OF SALVATION. EMBOLDEN US TO SHINE FOR YOU.

LET IT BE

Imagine that you were asked this question on a popular game show: *What is the most common phrase used to end a prayer?*

Even if you are not an active Christ follower, you most likely would be able to answer correctly without even having to "phone a friend" for help.

We have been conditioned to end our prayers with "amen," but do we understand what this phrase actually means? This Hebrew word is literally translated "let it be," stemming from the verb "to be firm or sure."

When the apostle Paul was instructing Timothy of God's impeccable timing, he inserted this prayer,

> *He is the only One who never dies. He lives in light*
> *so bright no one can go near it. No one has ever seen*
> *God, or can see Him. May honor and power belong*
> *to God forever. Amen (I Timothy 6:16 NCV).*

Paul describes God as both eternal and brilliantly bright. He gives us the impression that God's light is so bright that it's hard to see His features. That's how worthy of our honor and praise He is. The "amen" is the punctuation mark at the end of this, letting us know that we can be sure that this is so. Or in other words, *Let it be!*

This concept can also relate to us when we speak out His promises in our everyday lives.

God, You said that I am the apple of Your eye. *I am sure that I am.*

Jesus, You said to go and make disciples and with Your help I am willing to go. *Let it be!*

When we infuse our prayer life with this kind of belief, knowing that He is a firm and sure foundation, it can bolster our faith. Lord, let it be so!

GOD, WE TURN TO YOU AS OUR SURE AND FIRM FOUNDATION. WE WANT TO PRAY WITH CERTAINTY THAT YOU ARE FULLY IN CONTROL OF OUR LIVES. LET IT BE!

LIGHTS OUT

She could hear the sweet giggles of little girls coming from the bedroom down the hall and couldn't help but smile. How many times had she and her sister stayed up late into the night when they were young, telling stories and dreaming about what their future held? Countless.

Now that she had daughters of her own she relished the fact that they wanted to be close to one another, just as she and her sister had years ago. Soon they would be grown and would move into their own homes and start their own families, and the giggles wouldn't be as easy to come by. There would be heartaches to endure as they grew into the women who God had called them to be. They would walk through betrayals by friends, breakups with boyfriends, and a failed exam or two. But if they walked in the light, then they would have each other to lean on when the going got rough, and their love for each other would lift them up.

I John 2:10 (NIV) offers up this promise:

Anyone who loves their brother and sister lives in the light, and there is nothing in them to make them stumble.

The apostle John desired for those of us in the body of Christ to view each other as brothers and sisters, creating a close bond as we attempt to live each day in the light. He knew that there would be ups and downs in the days ahead, but through godly relationships we can be there for each other in the midst of both heartaches and celebrations, leaning on each other when our path seems unsteady, loving each other unconditionally.

As she kissed her daughter's round cheeks one last time and said, "Lights out, girls," the giggles started to quiet down. The lights might be out for the night, but their love for each other shone bright.

FATHER, LET US BE AN ENCOURAGEMENT TO OUR SISTERS AND BROTHERS AS WE WALK THROUGH THIS LIFE TOGETHER. MAY THEY FEEL YOUR LOVE SHINING THROUGH US.

BLAZING HEARTS

Do you remember the last time that your heart burned with passion for someone? At first you may have just felt that initial spark, but as you got to know that person more intimately, your spark turned into a full-fledged fire, burning within your heart. When you were apart, you most likely counted down the minutes until you could once again be with the one your heart desired.

Did you know that nothing gives God more pleasure than seeing our hearts ablaze with passion for Him and His Word?

After His resurrection, Jesus appeared to two individuals walking along the road to Emmaus. They did not recognize Jesus at first, but after breaking bread together their eyes were opened before He disappeared from their sight.

So they said to each other, "Weren't our hearts ablaze within us while He was talking with us on the road and explaining the Scriptures to us?" (Luke 24:32 HCSB)

How amazing it must have been to walk alongside the risen King and have the Scriptures explained in detail! Yet we have access to this very same encounter if we allow the Spirit to lead us and teach us His Word. The beauty of it all is that as we spend time in God's Word, it continues to ignite our passion for it. Just as a lamp is ignited by a single flame and keeps burning, so do our hearts as we burn with a desire to know Him more.

If you do not know this kind of blazing passion for God's Word, ask Him to ignite it within you. He is faithful to set your heart on fire!

JESUS, WE WANT NOTHING MORE THAN TO
KNOW YOU AND HAVE A BLAZING PASSION
FOR YOUR WORD. SET US ABLAZE TODAY.

FAITHFUL FRIENDS

Have you ever experienced paralysis in your life? The kind of paralysis where one debilitating episode comes after the other? You struggle to pick yourself up off the ground but to no avail.

And then you hear that there is a man in town who performs miracles. He goes by the name of Jesus; some are even calling Him the Son of God.

Your friends walk in and gently place you on a stretcher. They inform you that they are taking you to meet this Jesus. Yet just as your hope begins to soar, the realization that the chances of your friends getting you inside the jam-packed building to where your healing lies are slim to none. There is not an inch of room to spare.

But your friends are not ordinary. No. They are extra-ordinary.

They look at the seemingly impossible situation and find a way to climb the walls with you on the stretcher, remove part of the roof, and lower you into the room where the Son of God is teaching. Amazingly, you are placed at the very spot you need to be: in front of the only One who is capable of forgiving your sins and healing your limp body.

This is all because your friends saw your need as greater than their own. You know that they each have things they would like to ask of the Son of God. They could use miracles in their own lives, but their selflessness and desire to see you restored take precedence. They are faithful friends.

And Jesus, seeing *their* faith, grants the healing and forgiveness that you have desperately hoped for since the paralysis hit. Your healing comes because of the self-sacrificial love of your friends who were willing to do whatever it took to place you directly in front of your Savior.

Luke 5:20 NCV tells us,

> *Seeing their faith, Jesus said, "Friend,*
> *your sins are forgiven."*

Now that you are healed, will you do the same for others? Are you willing to be a faithful friend?

JESUS, WHAT A BLESSING IT IS TO HAVE
EXTRAORDINARY FRIENDS WHO SHOW US YOUR
LOVE. HELP US TO BE FAITHFUL FRIENDS TO OTHERS.

PACKING LIGHT

She had no clue how she was going to get herself packed for two weeks of travel for a business trip. It didn't help that her two destinations were sure to provide drastically different climates or that she needed to pack light. She tried all the tricks, rolling her clothes carefully, yet her suitcase kept bulging at the seams. She wondered if the airlines might miss the fact that her carry-on luggage weighed more than a baby elephant. Slim chance!

She backed away from the challenge for a few hours and came back with better perspective and new resolve to get the job done. After carefully considering the itinerary of each day, she found ways to reuse articles of clothing, giving the illusion that she had a new outfit for each day. As she closed her luggage for the last time, she was relieved to see that it zipped with ease.

In the Sermon on the Mount Jesus told His followers that they didn't need to worry about things such as clothing.

Why worry about your clothing? Look at the lilies of the field and how they grow. They don't work or make their clothing, yet Solomon in all his glory was not dressed as beautifully as they are. And if God cares so wonderfully for wildflowers that are here today and thrown into the fire tomorrow, He will certainly care for you. Why do you have so little faith? (Matthew 6:28–30 NLT)

Jesus is not against fashion. He just wants you to know that it's not worth worrying about. In fact, He doesn't want you to worry at all about anything, ever, because He is in control and He loves you.

We can take a lesson from the lilies of the field and know that He will care for us. Such realization gives us the freedom to start packing light.

JESUS, THANK YOU FOR CARING FOR US IN SUCH AN INTRICATE WAY THAT YOU DRESS US BETTER THAN THE LILIES OF THE FIELD. LET US BE WILLING TO PUT OUR FAITH IN YOU AND START PACKING LIGHT.

THERE IS THE
RADIANCE OF THE
SUN AND DIFFERING
RADIANCE FOR
THE MOON AND
FOR THE STARS.
EVEN THE STARS
DIFFER IN THEIR
SHINING.

I Corinthians 15:41 TPT

GET TO!

There's a Christian camp tucked away in the pine trees of Texas where the counselors have this motto: *We don't "have to"; we "GET TO!"*

As they go about their everyday activities, they have the attitude of "I get to do this!" rather than "I have to do this."

For instance, they have a mindset of "I GET the joy of playing with a dozen three-year-olds for hours on end," rather than "I can't believe I have to swelter in this heat with these crazy kids." Or, "I simply cannot wait to rise to lead you on a ten-mile bike ride" versus "You mean I have to wake up at the crack of dawn? I'll be exhausted before lunch."

It's simply a mind-over-matter proposition. When they tell themselves they are living a privileged life then they exude joy instead of grumbling, and they have a sense of peace instead of entitlement, all while doing the very same activity!

We too can have a positive attitude when it comes to our everyday lives. Will we choose to adopt the attitude of we "get to" rise early and spend time with the One who created us, or will we begrudgingly get out of bed, feeling that if we don't we will be judged by others? Will we choose to joyfully serve those less fortunate than us or will we complain through the whole activity?

The state of our mind is also important to the Almighty:

For the mindset of the flesh is death, but the mindset
of the Spirit is life and peace (Romans 8:6 LEB).

Isn't it neat that the result of living a "get to" kind of life is that we have a life filled with peace? What a blessing it is to be privileged with a lifestyle of peace while getting to do all the things that He has called us to do. And the best part is we don't "have to"; we "GET TO!"

GOD, THANK YOU FOR EVERY OPPORTUNITY
TO "GET TO" DO THE THINGS THAT YOU HAVE
CALLED US TO DO. WE DON'T EVER WANT TO
TAKE YOUR BLESSINGS FOR GRANTED.

SHINE AND SEEK

Do you remember playing the game of hide-and-seek when you were a child? One person was deemed "it" while the others hid in their best spots. As the game went on, the others would join in the hunt once they were found. The holdout would be left trying to suppress his laughter lest he be caught next. When the final "gotcha" was given, squeals of joy would reverberate through the house until the parents hollered to "keep it down." You could feel the happiness in the air as you whiled the hours away.

Guess what? The Lord is ready to reignite that feeling of happiness inside you as you play a little game of "shine and seek" with Him. The psalmist lays out the rules of the game in Psalm 105:3–4 (TPT),

> *Shine and make your joyful boast in Him,*
> *you lovers of God. Let's be happy and*
> *keep rejoicing no matter what. Seek more*
> *of His strength! Seek more of Him! Let's*
> *always be seeking the light of His face.*

Rule Number 1: On your mark, get set, SHINE! As women who love God, we don't hide from Him but rather allow His light and joy to infuse us to the point of rejoicing, no matter what, meaning that we find our satisfaction and our contentment in Him alone.

Rule Number 2: You're "it"! He wants you to seek Him with your whole heart…never giving up. Seek His strength for whatever you're going through in this moment. Seek His wisdom to make wise decisions. Seek the light of His face and allow it to illuminate your whole life.

That's how you win at this game of life, when you shine and seek!

LORD, WE EARNESTLY SEEK YOUR LIGHT
TODAY, KNOWING THAT AS YOU ARE
FOUND, WE ARE ABLE TO SHINE!

YOUR LIFE MATTERS

Do you believe that your life matters?

With over seven and a half billion people living on planet earth, it's sometimes easy to think that our life is insignificant in the grand scheme of things. We may be tempted to think, *Who is really going to miss us in a world this big?* But that is not what God says.

He says in Ephesians 1:4 (The Message),

Long before He laid down earth's foundations, He had us in mind, had settled on us as the focus of His love.

If we truly believe that God's Word is true, then how can we not think that our life matters when He tells us that we are the focus of His love?

But what is even more amazing is how He loved us BEFORE the earth was even created. He knew that we would be right where we are, shining His light and living as His beloved before this big, crazy world even existed. What a mind-blowing yet comforting concept!

But that's not all! It says that we will be made whole and holy by His love. No matter how broken you feel today by life's recent events, or how unworthy of love you may think that you are, God says that His love will restore you to a sense of wholeness and holiness.

He has a specific purpose and plan for your life. The focus of the God of the universe is on you individually, and He loves you beyond anything that you can do or imagine. Your life matters to Him and it always will.

GOD, WE RECEIVE YOUR LOVE AND ALLOW IT TO RESTORE US TO A PLACE OF WHOLENESS TODAY. THANK YOU FOR SETTING ME AS YOUR FOCUS BEFORE THE EARTH WAS EVEN CREATED. IT IS A BEAUTIFUL THING TO KNOW THAT OUR LIVES MATTER TO YOU.

BRIGHT AND BEAUTIFUL STRENGTH

God made it so that work is one of the most fulfilling things that we can do while on earth. We gain satisfaction from a job well done, and more often than not, friendships are formed in the workplace, making our jobs more pleasurable.

Yet there are seasons of life when we can work ourselves to a nub and the thing that we most enjoyed about our profession feels insurmountable. We start making mistakes on the job, which leads to bad reviews. Or we have an altercation with a coworker that makes meetings with them awkward. Sure, we may be able to grit our teeth and endure for a while, but soon we find our strength is zapped and showing up for work feels unendurable.

The apostle Paul found that some church members were feeling this same way, so he sent these words to encourage them,

As you learn more and more how God works, you will learn how to do your work. We pray that you'll have the strength to stick it out over the long haul—not the grim strength of gritting your teeth but the glory-strength God gives (Colossians 1:11–12 The Message).

But that's not all! He goes on to tell about this "glory-strength",

It is strength that endures the unendurable and spills over into joy, thanking the Father who makes us strong enough to take part in everything bright and beautiful that He has for us (Colossians 1:11-12 The Message).

God didn't intend for us to grin and bear our work but to have true joy in the workplace. We achieve this by doing things in His strength, not our own. And the beauty of it all is that when we do, bright and beautiful things are in store for us!

GOD, YOU ARE LORD OVER OUR WORK.
WE ASK FOR YOUR GLORY-STRENGTH AS
WE SEEK TO DO OUR JOBS WITH JOY.

THE ILLUMINATED
PATH OF FELLOWSHIP

What does it mean to "walk in the light"? Would it surprise you to know that part of walking in the light is having fellowship with other believers?

In I John 1:7, it says,

> *if we walk in the light then we have*
> *fellowship with one another.*

This word fellowship is *koinonia*, meaning "sharing, unity, close association, a communion." It is a unity brought about by the Holy Spirit. *Koinonia* cements the believers to the Lord Jesus and to each other. After Peter delivered his compelling "repent and be baptized" sermon in Acts 2, Scripture tells us that the believers had this special kind of fellowship with each other.

When God put us here on earth, He never intended for us to walk through life alone. He wants us to share our lives with others, which means we celebrate the successes of our friends and cry through their struggles. When we find out our girlfriend has cancer, we rally around her and lay hands on her in prayer. When we hear that our brother has lost his job, we take his family a meal and lend him a listening ear. All the while, our hearts are being cemented to each other and to our relationship with the Lord.

Walking in the light was never supposed to be an individual path with just you and God. Walking the illuminated path means that we share our light with our brothers and sisters when they need it and they do the same for us, causing our cumulative light to shine even brighter.

Extend your light to a friend today and walk the illuminated path of fellowship.

FATHER, THANK YOU FOR THE GIFT OF FELLOWSHIP
AND HOW IT CEMENTS US TO EACH OTHER AND
TO YOU. PUT SOMEONE IN OUR PATH TODAY
WHOM WE CAN ILLUMINATE WITH YOUR LIGHT.

BLINDED BY THE LIGHT

Has God ever gone to extreme measures to get your attention?

Perhaps you were marching through life to the beat of your own drum when the next thing you knew everything went dark and you ended up flat on your face with your head spinning. *So much for that still, small voice,* you think to yourself. *What just happened?!*

Before the apostle Paul had his conversion, he was known as Saul, persecutor of the Christians. He was ruthless in his pursuit of righteousness, believing that he was defending God while ridding the world of Christ-followers. That is until he was blinded by the Light!

The Book of Acts recounts the story of Jesus appearing to him on the road to Damascus and describes His presence as

*a light from heaven, brighter than
the sun (Acts 26:13 NIV).*

Jesus blinded Saul that day in order to fully gain his attention. He knew the plans that He had for Saul (soon to be Paul) and for his followers, called Christians. He knew that they would need to start working together so that the gospel could reach the world, and in order for that to happen, Paul had to start to see things in full light.

The same is true in our everyday lives. It could be that we truly believe that what we are doing is right and just, until we hold it up to the light of truth and we realize that it is we who need the conversion, not the other way around. Sometimes we have to be blinded by the Light in order to fully see His plan and be effective for spreading the gospel of Jesus Christ. But when our heads stop spinning and our vision returns, watch out, because we are going to light this world up!

JESUS, BRING TO LIGHT THE SPACES OF
DARKNESS IN OUR LIVES. LIGHT US UP
FOR THE SAKE OF THE GOSPEL!

JUST SPARKLE

We all have a story to share that can potentially help someone else. Each one of us has gone through various trials, and if we allow the Lord to lead us through them, then most likely we can come out with a story that, when told, will glorify our Father in heaven.

Imagine yourself as a sparkler. If you have accepted Christ as your Savior, then He sent His fire to light your sparkler to burn brightly for Him. As you sparkle, your light is attractive to others, increasing their curiosity about what sparked the flame in you to begin with.

Yet the enemy hates the light inside of you, so he comes with his lies of darkness. *What makes you think you're special? Why would anyone listen to your story? That person knew you at your worst; why would she believe you're a new creation? You better just hide that light of yours and keep quiet.*

But hear this, dear friend: Light always dispels the darkness. It is not your job to create the light. That's already been done by Someone far more powerful. It is your job to testify about the light and just sparkle.

The Bible describes John the Baptist in this way,

> *This man came as a witness, to testify about the Light, so that all might believe [in Christ, the Light] through him (John 1:7 AMP).*

John knew that his job was to make the light that was inside of him visible to all so that they would believe in a power that was greater than him. As he testified (shared his story), many were attracted to the light and believed!

We too have this opportunity to make the light visible in our everyday lives. Share your story. Just sparkle.

> FATHER, ALLOW US TO SPARKLE SO BRIGHTLY
> THAT OTHERS ARE ATTRACTED TO YOU.
> GIVE US THE COURAGE TO SHARE OUR
> STORY AND TESTIFY ABOUT THE LIGHT.

FOUND BY THE LIGHT

D o you remember getting in trouble as a little child? Perhaps you would run and hide, thinking that you could outsmart your parents. You thought, *If I can just stay still long enough in the dark closet, maybe they'll forget about what I've done.* Yet for some reason that never seemed to work out. The minute you shifted, on came the lights and your hiding self was exposed. How did they know? You were so stealthy…

King David had these very same thoughts. Psalm 139:11–12 (NLT) gives great voice to how deeply our Creator knows us:

> *I could ask the darkness to hide me and the light around me to become night—but even in darkness I cannot hide from You. To You the night shines as bright as day. Darkness and light are the same to You.*

David knew that it was useless to try to hide from the very One who called his being into existence. Because He is light, the darkness could never conceal David from the Lord's presence.

The same applies to us as children of the light. It is not a place to be scared of, but rather it is the most wonderful and secure place to be. The Lord offers us forgiveness from our mistakes, strength when we feel as if we may fail, and light when our world seems dark and overwhelming.

When we allow ourselves to be found by the light, we are privy to all His benefits, just as cherished children are in their secure homes. It's a home filled with His presence and His light.

LORD, HELP US TO SEE THAT THE DARKNESS NEVER OFFERS US THE SAME BENEFITS AS BEING FOUND BY THE LIGHT. YOU ARE A GOOD FATHER TO US.

BURNING BRIDGES

The past can be a sneaky thing, can't it? The minute you think you've dealt with everything, it comes creeping back in…reminding you of your failures…threatening to take you down again.

But then you remember that you serve a God who says that He casts your sin as far as the east is from the west and that He is there to give you a good and prosperous future. Once you've repented of your sin, you don't need to live in the past anymore. In fact, it's time to burn that bridge once and for all.

The apostle Paul knew what it was like to live with a past that was less than stellar. There were many things that he participated in that were cringe-worthy, but instead of dwelling on them, he resolved to fasten his heart to the future instead.

Paul tells us exactly how to burn those bridges in Philippians 3:13 (TPT),

I don't depend on my own strength to accomplish this; however I do have one compelling focus: I forget all of the past as I fasten my heart to the future instead.

First, we light the match, not in our own strength, but in God's never-ending strength. Then as we set fire to the past, we intentionally turn our eyes away from the blaze. It's then we know turning back to our old ways would be a waste of time and energy. After all, that bridge is completely burned down. It's time to focus elsewhere.

So, we fix our eyes on the brightness of the future that lies ahead, and with every step we take the burn of the past becomes a distant memory. No more regrets. Our hearts are fastened to the light.

JESUS, DO FOR US WHAT YOU DID FOR PAUL. HELP US TO BURN THE BRIDGES OF THE PAST AND FASTEN OUR HEARTS TO THE FUTURE YOU HAVE FOR US.

KEEP
SHINING,
BEAUTIFUL ONE.
THE WORLD
NEEDS YOUR
LIGHT.

ANONYMOUS

A JOYFUL HEART

She had read a vast number of the parenting books on the market but was still struggling with getting her strong-willed son to obey with a joyful heart. More often than not he would consent and eventually obey the command given to him, but there was a permanent scowl attached to his small face. She exhaled deeply and wondered what to do. She knew that in his underdeveloped mind he was thinking: *I'm technically doing what you asked of me, so why does it matter what my attitude is?* But to her it mattered a great deal. It was a heart issue.

Days later she was meeting with her Bible study group. The conversation turned to the importance of our attitude as we follow Christ. The Shepherd said that He would lead us in paths of righteousness, but He never said He intended for us to come along with our arms crossed and our lips turned out in a pout.

A light bulb went off in her heart in that moment as she remembered the Scripture in Psalm 97:11 NLT:

> *Light shines on the godly, and joy on*
> *those whose hearts are right.*

She both surrendered her attitude and asked for guidance on how to better lead her son into obedience.

Just as she would prefer that her son have a joyful heart as he follows her instruction, Jesus prefers the same from us. He wants our hearts to be right first and foremost, knowing that only then are we in a position to receive His blessings.

That doesn't mean that the path will be easy. In fact, living a godly life takes a lot of self-sacrifice. But along that path we find a life of joy and light.

JESUS, YOU ARE THE GOOD SHEPHERD WHO LOVES
US UNCONDITIONALLY. YET YOU DESIRE FOR US TO
WALK IN OBEDIENCE TO YOUR COMMANDS WITH
A JOYFUL HEART. HELP US TO GET OUR HEARTS
RIGHT AND LET YOUR LIGHT SHINE ON US ALWAYS.

LOVE SO SUPREME

The silence was deafening. Neither she nor her husband wanted to be the first to speak.

They had driven like this for miles, both of them staring out the window, unwilling to make eye contact. Until… with one sweeping motion his hand reached across the great divide of the console and found her hand. As their fingers intertwined the tension seemed to melt away. It wasn't long before the "I'm sorrys" came tumbling out of both of their hearts and mouths.

In Colossians 3, the apostle Paul reminds us that because we have been graciously forgiven by Jesus, we should be willing to release this same gift to others. He says,

> *Tolerate the weaknesses of those in the family of faith, forgiving one another in the same way you have been graciously forgiven by Jesus Christ. If you find fault with someone, realize this same gift of forgiveness to them. For love is supreme and must flow through each of these virtues. Love becomes the mark of true maturity (3:13–14 TPT).*

As we walk in the light, maturity starts to mark us in such a way that love begins to reign supreme. It's not that we don't still have ample opportunities to exercise the gift of forgiveness because real-life relationships are messy. As conflicts arise, we can feel justified in our "fault-finding" and harbor unforgiveness. Or we can reach our hand across the console and release the hurt, replacing it with love, just as Jesus did for us.

True maturity comes when we are willing to do the hard things. It's then that we are marked by love and we can demonstrate to others that love is indeed supreme.

JESUS, THANK YOU FOR THE GRACE-FILLED
FORGIVENESS THAT YOU LAVISHED ON US.
HELP US TO FOLLOW YOUR EXAMPLE AND
EXTEND THE GIFT OF FORGIVENESS TO OTHERS,
ALLOWING LOVE TO REIGN SUPREME IN US.

A RAY OF BRIGHTNESS

As she opened her sleepy eyes, she was instantly greeted by a ray of brightness shining through the Colorado cabin window, showing off the beauty of a snowcapped mountain.

Because she had driven in late the night before, the majestic scenery was hidden in the darkness. But now at first light, God's creation was revealed in all its splendor. As she took a moment to breathe in the fresh mountain air, she remembered a day not too long ago when she prayed that the Lord would steady her faith.

She had been feeling unsure of His promises and could feel herself drifting and even a little distant from God. But seeing the mountains that the Lord had created, she felt grounded, secure, stable.

For times such as these, it's a blessing to have God's Word. King David found comfort in the Lord and His creation in Psalm 18:2 (TPT),

You're as real to me as bedrock beneath my feet...
my mountain of hiding...my secret strength...You are
salvation's ray of brightness shining on the hillside.

David knew what it felt like to be on unsteady ground, but he also knew who could provide the strength and stability he so desired. As he put his faith in the Lord, he was able to experience salvation as a ray of brightness, allowing God to shed His light on his situation. He could feel the Lord's presence as real as the bedrock beneath his feet.

If you find yourself on unsteady ground, ask the Lord of all creation to shine His ray of brightness on your situation. No issue you may have is too big or small for Him. He is as real as the ground beneath your feet and He will be your secret strength.

LORD, WE NEED YOUR VERY REAL AND
POWERFUL PRESENCE TO GROUND OUR FAITH.
WHEN WE FEEL UNSTEADY, YOU ARE THE
BEDROCK BENEATH OUR FEET. COME SHINE
YOUR RAY OF BRIGHTNESS ON US TODAY.

DO IT, LORD

They ended their time together at Bible study by fervently praying over one of their friends, who was hitting some roadblocks in the process of adopting her daughter.

As a group of women, they had all invested in bringing this sweet girl home from Ethiopia by fundraising and praying for the process for several months now. They were not about to let some paperwork hang-ups prevent this precious child from being with her forever family! So they did the only thing that they knew to do, and that was to call upon the name of the One who could get the job done.

The prayer time came to a close with much enthusiasm. The women stood in agreement and said, "Do it, Lord! Do it!"

And guess what? He did it! Within a few months their friends were headed to Africa to get their girl. Much celebration followed. God heard their prayers and they praised Him for answering.

Jeremiah 32:17 NIV says,

Ah, Sovereign Lord, You have made the heavens and the earth by Your great power and outstretched arm. Nothing is too hard for You.

It pleases God when we pray with boldness and recall His great power. Does that mean that He will always answer our prayers the exact way that we think He should? Not at all. But that should not stop us from asking Him to do things on our behalf.

Perhaps you are in a season of life right now where you are fervently praying for God to move on your behalf. Maybe it's for a financial breakthrough or physical healing or the homecoming of a child whom you have prayed countless prayers for.

Whatever it may be, call upon His name not in fear but in faith! After all, nothing is too hard for Him.

Do it, Lord!

SOVEREIGN LORD, NOTHING IS TOO HARD FOR YOU. WE CALL UPON YOUR NAME TO ACT ON OUR BEHALF AND WE GIVE YOU ALL THE GLORY.

THE ART OF HUMILITY

Humility. This word is rarely the hot topic at dinner parties, or even sermon series for that matter. We would rather talk about *anything* other than being humble because that's so blah. How can we be made to shine when we are called to live a life of humility?

When we open this leather-bound thing we call the Bible, we find that Jesus modeled the art of humility perfectly for us (and He was the essence of shiny while doing so!). He is the King of kings and Lord of lords, yet He showed up on this earth and slept in a feeding trough for animals. He allowed Himself to be baptized in the muddy Jordan River by His cousin. He rode on a donkey instead of a horse. He washed His disciples' dirty feet. He died on a criminal's cross.

Yet at every turn His life-giving light spilled out onto everyone He came into contact with. He wasn't concerned with being exalted in those moments; He was more concerned with showing us what a truly humble servant looks like.

Paul sums up Christ's humility perfectly in Philippians 2 by saying that even though He was God, He took on the very nature of a servant and humbled Himself. So much so that He became obedient to death on a cross, which was the most humiliating thing that a person could have done in that day and age!

Therefore God exalted Him to the highest
place and gave Him the name that is above
every name (Philippians 2:9 NIV).

The art of humility doesn't mean that we are self-deprecating or a doormat for the world to wipe their feet on. Rather, it means changing the world by simply loving like Jesus loved and shining His light with every foot that we are willing to wash.

JESUS, MAKE US HUMBLE LIKE YOU. TEACH US
THE ART OF HUMILITY AND LET US CONSIDER
OTHERS BETTER THAN OURSELVES.

OUR PEACE

In a world filled with conflict, a life of peace sounds sublime right about now.

Day after day we hear the news reports. They are filled with such violence and discord, leaving so many hurting and grieving. Lives are forever changed in an instant and we are left shaking our heads, wondering what in the world the answer is.

The answer is peace. More specifically, the answer is found in THE Person who embodies peace.

Micah 5:5 (NLT) says of the Anointed One,

He will be the source of peace.

When our security is threatened: He is our peace. When our best friend betrays us: He is our peace. When we miscarry our baby: He is our peace.

Jesus never promised that our lives would be filled with days of abundant sunshine. In fact, He specifically said that in this world, we WILL have many trials and sorrows, but to take heart because He has overcome the world (John 16:33). That's a promise that we can hold onto when our world is shaken.

But we can't miss the first part of that promise. Jesus specifically says, "I have told you these things, so that IN

ME you may HAVE PEACE" (John 16:33 NIV, emphasis added). Without Jesus, we would have no sense of peace. He is the reason we can "take heart" even in the midst of heartbreaking situations.

So the next time that life feels uncertain and we don't know what to do, we extend our hand and take hold of His, allowing His peace to wash over us. Our almighty God knows exactly what we need and He freely gives it to us. He is our source of peace.

JESUS, WE NEED YOU TO BE NEAR TO US IN OUR TIME OF HEARTBREAK AND PROVIDE US WITH THE PEACE THAT ONLY YOU CAN PROVIDE. TEACH US TO HOLD ON TO YOUR PROMISES AND TURN TO YOU.

REFRESH

Tired. Run down. Spiritually dry. Do any of these words describe you right now?

It's easy to feel like we are in the hamster wheel of life, spinning constantly but never going anywhere. It's not long before our little legs give out and we fall out on the wood chips. The trap is that we convince ourselves that we are too busy to take any time for ourselves to be still before God. And you can just forget about serving others. There just aren't enough hours in the day for such activities. Before we know it we're physically exhausted, emotionally spent, and spiritually dull and dry.

God understands that our lives can be spiritually depleting, therefore, He told us how to be refreshed so that we can shine once again:

The generous will prosper; those who refresh others will themselves be refreshed (Proverbs 11:25 NLT).

Generosity comes in all shapes and sizes. We can be generous with our love, our home, our time, our money. The point is to be a person who is known for her giving in her everyday life activities.

Pick up the phone and ask that friend who is struggling in her faith to go to lunch this week. Or buy an extra cup of coffee and give it to your child's teacher or the security guard who holds the door open for you at work. By recognizing simple ways to refresh others, we find that we too begin feeling refreshed.

As we start to make that wheel of generosity spin rather than the meaningless wheel of exhaustion, we find that we are being filled with God's all-refreshing power. And before we know it, the dullness has diminished and our shine is back!

FATHER, LET US BE WOMEN WHO ARE KNOWN
FOR OUR GENEROSITY. PROVIDE US WITH AN
OPPORTUNITY TODAY TO REFRESH ONE OF
YOUR CHILDREN. MAKE US SHINE FOR YOU!

SHAME UNDONE

Shame. It's a small word, but it carries a power-packed punch.

What makes shame so powerful is that it is both debilitating and universal, meaning that not one of us is unaffected by its devastating effects.

Shame has destroyed marriages, orphaned children, bankrupted souls, and even taken countless lives. The shrapnel that it slings into our hearts and minds tells us that we can never be free, that our shame can never be undone. So we live hopeless, helpless lives, completely blinded by our shame.

The apostle Paul speaks of such blinding shame in II Corinthians 4:4 (TPT),

> *Their blindness keeps them from seeing*
> *the dayspring light of the wonderful*
> *news of the glory of Jesus Christ,*
> *who is the divine image of God.*

How does one allow the dayspring light to enter while bound to shame? Paul says that the answer is to reject shame and turn to the truth. Jesus alone holds the power to undo our shame. No sin is too great for Him. He died for every single one of them.

When we view our shame in light of the gospel of Jesus Christ, our blindness dissipates and we see it for what it is, a chain holding us in darkness. But when we come face-to-face with Jesus we encounter brilliant dawning light that comes to speak directly to our shame and remove it from our lives. Marriages are restored. Children are adopted. Souls are invested in the knowledge of God.

His dayspring light sets us free and our shame is undone.

JESUS, HOW MAGNIFICENT IS YOUR DAYSPRING LIGHT THAT REMOVES OUR BLINDING SHAME AND REPLACES IT WITH EYES TO SEE YOU. LET YOUR BRILLIANT LIGHT SHINE OUT OF DARKNESS. TAKE OUR SHAME AND LET IT BE UNDONE IN YOUR NAME.

NOT TO US

In today's society it's easy to get caught up in our own little worlds. Perhaps we've had some success on the job and as the "congratulations" come rolling in, our heads start to swell a little. Or we post a picture of our children's accomplishments on social media and people are truly impressed with them. We don't mean for it to happen, but before we know it we are checking our app every ten seconds to see how many "likes" we've received. It's not that it's necessarily "wrong," it's just that it becomes self-focused. Left to our own devices, we can even take it as far as allowing the lack of "likes" by our "friends" to send us into a downward spiral, doubting our perceived influence on this world at large.

It's then that we need a shift in our perspective!

As humans there will always be the tendency to want the glory for ourselves. Again, it's not that we intentionally desire for these things to happen, but as we get a little taste of the glory, we get all heady and we want more and more until we have pushed God totally out of the picture. But if we are wise and we allow His light to illuminate the more excellent path, we can get back on track and give glory where glory is due.

Psalm 115:1 (NIV) says,

Not to us, LORD, not to us but to
Your name be the glory.

It is because of His love and faithfulness that we are even alive to live this illuminated life; therefore, He deserves the glory, not us. So, the next time we feel the urge to hold onto that glory for ourselves, we put this psalm on repeat: *Not to us, but to Your name be the glory.*

GOD, WE ARE SORRY WHEN WE HAVE TAKEN THE GLORY FOR OURSELVES. WE SAY, "NOT TO US, BUT TO YOUR NAME BE GLORY FOREVER AND EVER!"

DARKNESS
CANNOT DRIVE
OUT DARKNESS;
ONLY LIGHT CAN
DO THAT. HATE
CANNOT DRIVE OUT
HATE; ONLY LOVE
CAN DO THAT.

MARTIN LUTHER KING, JR.

ARISE AND SHINE

S he hadn't always been an early riser. In fact, her motto was, "The more beauty rest, the better."

However, there are only so many hours in a day, and even though she was fully rested, she began to feel sluggish and spiritually depleted. Why? Because she was neglecting the One who holds the power to totally and completely fill her, thus missing out on His soul-satisfying presence.

She had a life-altering conversation with a friend in a similar season of life who encouraged her to set her alarm an hour earlier and ask the Holy Spirit to wake her up. And guess what? He did!

Now she craves that time at first light when it is just her and her Creator, spending time in His Word, gaining wisdom on how to be a better wife, mother, sister, and daughter. Telling the Lord of her struggles and experiencing His sweet encouragement. It's there that she also asks for opportunities to reflect the light of Christ in her everyday life.

God told the Israelites in Isaiah 60:1 (HCSB) after a long period of spiritual dryness,

Arise, shine, for your light has come, and the glory of the Lord shines over you.

Notice that they first had to arise if they wanted to shine. They wouldn't have been able to experience the full glory of the Almighty by staying in their comfortable tents, and we won't either. But He wants us to know that it is worth every minute of lost beauty rest. In fact, being willing to arise will make us more beautiful.

The specific hour of the day isn't as important as simply being willing to consistently arise in order to spend time with the One who makes us shine!

LORD, WE DESIRE FOR YOUR GLORY TO SHINE OVER US. WE UNDERSTAND THE IMPORTANCE OF ARISING TO MEET WITH YOU SO THAT WE CAN BE THE BEST VERSION OF OURSELVES. WAKE US UP TO ARISE AND SHINE.

BUILD OTHERS UP

With a single word we have the ability to build someone up or tear them down.

It's not hard to know how people are feeling these days with the constant flow of comments across social media. Most of the time, the posts are pleasant and even uplifting and it's enjoyable to give a double-tap heart of approval. But occasionally there's a comment that makes the stiffest of jaws drop at the person's insensitivity to a particular topic. We wonder why in the world they decided it would be a good idea to voice their opinion so rudely for all the world to see. Didn't their mama teach them better?

Yet when we take the time to examine our own speech, we need to be cognizant of how often we offer a critical word instead of an encouraging one. This is especially important in areas of marriage and parenting. Oftentimes it is easier to point out what our spouses and/or children aren't doing rather than praise them for what they *are* doing.

Ephesians 4:29 (The Message) says,

Watch the way you talk. Let nothing foul or dirty come out of your mouth. Say only what helps, each word a gift.

Whoa! That's convicting for sure.

When we think about the words that we speak as being a gift, it should influence the way we talk. We wouldn't hand our loved ones some dirty, wadded-up paper towels and expect them to think that we were actually presenting them with a gift. Nor would we want to receive such a "gift."

So, the next time we open our mouths to correct our children, address our spouse, or type out that response online, let's resolve to build others up, not tear them down.

HOLY SPIRIT, THANK YOU FOR THE REMINDER
TO BUILD EACH OTHER UP WITH OUR WORDS,
PRESENTING THEM WITH THE SWEETEST OF GIFTS.

THE MELDING OF PATIENCE
AND COURAGE

How many times have we heard the saying "Patience is a virtue"? However, patience, for most of us, is not our favorite discipline to practice. Our drive-thru mentality has made certain of that.

But what if instant gratification is not an option for our particular situation? It could be that we are waiting on test results and are at the mercy of our doctor's staff. Or maybe we are waiting on a callback for a job interview we recently had. Possibly we find ourselves waiting for reconciliation to happen with a fractured relationship.

Real life is often complicated, and we don't have nearly the control we think that we do to make the timing fit our schedule. We anxiously stare at the clock and somewhat respectfully ask the Lord to hurry up and answer us. In times like these, it's important for us to be able to turn to God's Word and realize that patience is actually God-ordained.

James 5:8 (NLT) tells us,

> *You, too, must be patient. Take courage,*
> *for the coming of the Lord is near.*

Just as a farmer has to wait on the spring rains in order to produce a good crop, we too must be patient with our circumstances, knowing that in time God will work it out for our best, if we trust in Him.

So the next time you're in a season of waiting, let your heart take courage and be patient through the long days. God is always near to us and He's got it all under control.

FATHER, WE'RE SORRY ABOUT OUR IMPATIENT
NATURE AND ASK FOR YOU TO REPLACE IT
WITH PATIENCE AND COURAGE AS WE WAIT
ON YOU. WE BELIEVE YOU ARE NEAR, AND WE
WANT NOTHING MORE THAN YOUR PRESENCE
TO INFILTRATE OUR HEARTS AND MINDS.

GOD WITH US

One of the most personal and magnificent names for Jesus is Immanuel, God with us.

When Joseph was visited by the angel of the Lord, he was told this,

> *"She will give birth to a son, and you are to give Him the name Jesus, because He will save His people from their sins." All this took place to fulfill what the Lord had said through the prophet: "The virgin will conceive and give birth to a son, and they will call Him Immanuel" (which means "God with us") (Matthew 1:21–22 NIV).*

This name for Jesus brings comfort to mankind because it suggests His continued presence. It wasn't just that Jesus lived on the earth more than two thousand years ago and existed only then. No. He is with us, day in and day out, just as God intended from the beginning. God had manifest Himself in human flesh for the purpose of our deliverance. Could any gift be any sweeter?

We have the same opportunity in the twenty-first century to invite the presence of the Almighty into our homes just as Joseph and Mary did all those years ago. However, it will require intentionality on our part if we want Him to take up full residence within us.

We do this by talking to Him every day, seeking His advice on how to live our lives, and placing Him at the forefront of our conversations. We allow Him to truly dwell with us, and our relationship with Him is authentic and comfortable. We tell others of how He came to save us from our sins and His gift of salvation is free to all. Before long we find that He has totally permeated our entire being and His presence never leaves us.

He is Immanuel, God with us each and every day.

IMMANUEL, YOU ARE WELCOME IN OUR HEARTS AND OUR HOMES. COME DWELL WITH US DAILY.

AN ENLIGHTENED LIFE

It's common for us to feel from time to time as if we are sleepwalking through this life of ours. We may have experienced trauma and retreated to what we deemed a safe place. Or it could be that we simply feel as if things are happening around us but we are not actively participating in any of them.

The danger is that sleepwalking can become a coping mechanism that, if left unattended, can rob us of a full life. A life that God never intended for us to live.

God wants us to live an enLIGHTened life, one where our hearts are totally flooded with His light. In order for this to happen we have to obtain an inner awareness of who we are in Him. Ephesians 1:18 (NLT) tells us,

> *I pray that your hearts will be flooded with light*
> *so that you can understand the confident hope*
> *He has given to those He called—His holy people*
> *who are His rich and glorious inheritance.*

He says that we are His holy people, His rich and glorious inheritance, and we should handle ourselves accordingly.

Imagine you had a sports car that you wanted to give to your spouse. Yet when you gave him the keys, he immediately parked it in the garage and never allowed anyone to go near it. You would no doubt feel disappointed that he never fully enjoyed the gift you gave him.

The same applies to us in our everyday lives. We need to wake up and enjoy the enlightened life so that we can understand the calling that He has on our lives. We are never going to reach anyone with the gospel and offer them the same confident hope that we have by parking ourselves in the garage. But if we allow our hearts to be flooded with His light, then we can't help but shine everywhere we go!

FATHER, ALLOW OUR HEARTS TO BE FLOODED WITH YOUR LIGHT. WAKE US UP TO SHARE ABOUT THE CONFIDENT HOPE THAT ONLY YOU PROVIDE. THANK YOU FOR CALLING US TO AN ENLIGHTENED LIFE.

STARTING AGAIN

Do you remember your first date? Getting all dolled up, stressing over the perfect outfit and shade of lipstick? Anxiously wondering, *Will he like me? Will I like him? What will we talk about? Will he hold my hand?* Ahhh, the memories of young love.

But if we've lived more than a minute, we know that love relationships aren't all bouquets of roses every day. As a relationship progresses, there is always a risk that it will lead into "heartbreak valley." We find that we can't control the other person's actions, and the possibility of having our hearts broken is a very real thing.

The same can be said of life in general. There are valleys that we walk through that are filled with painful memories and darkness. The temptation is to sit down and give up, letting our tears carry us deeper and deeper into the valley. But God says that He's not willing for you to stay there. He nudges us to get up and start again. So He shines His light so that we can find the acres of hope that we desperately need. Hosea 2:16 (The Message) tells us,

And now, here's what I'm going to do... I'll turn Heartbreak Valley into Acres of Hope.

It's not an easy walk out of Heartbreak Valley and into Acres of Hope. In fact, it will require much soul-searching and prayer, a relinquishing of control and a willingness to replace it with trust in a greater plan than ours. Yet it's there that we are wooed once again with bouquets of roses and we remember our First Love. Brush yourself off, beautiful one, and start walking toward the light. It's time to start again.

LORD, YOU ARE OUR FIRST LOVE, THE ONE
WHO SHINES THE LIGHT IN OUR DARKEST
VALLEY AND LEADS US TO ACRES OF HOPE.
WE PUT OUR TRUST IN YOU ALONE.

HYDRATE TO DOMINATE

If you've ever played sports in your lifetime, then you know how important it is to be fully hydrated. If you start the game without much water in you, you'll start to feel faint and even cramp up, which can take you out of the game altogether. But if you start the game fully hydrated and you diligently replenish your fluids as you play, you will be a far better competitor. Thus the saying, "Hydrate to dominate!"

The same is true in the game of life. If we want to play hard then we better be fully hydrated from the start. Spiritually speaking, this concept was taught by Jesus Himself. He said,

All you thirsty ones, come to Me! Come to Me and drink! Believe in Me so that rivers of living water will burst out from within you, flowing from your innermost being, just like the Scripture says! (John 7:37–38 TPT).

If we are going to be effective for the Kingdom, then we need to be filled with living water that comes by having a relationship with Jesus…believing in Him as our Lord and Savior. But the thing about thirst is that it keeps coming back as we exert our energy. So, we can't just fill up on His living water once and expect it to last our whole lifetime, but rather we keep coming back to replenish as life goes on.

And the cool part about it is, the more we keep coming back to hydrate, the more unquenchable our thirst becomes until we ourselves are bursting with living water, sloshing it out on whomever is in the game with us! That's how we dominate in life, by hydrating with His living water.

JESUS, WE ARE THIRSTY. WE WANT MORE OF YOU.
HYDRATE US SO FULLY WITH YOUR LIVING WATER
THAT IF FLOWS FROM OUR INNERMOST BEING.

WALKING ON AIR

Have you ever begged God for something specific only to see Him give it to someone else? It's even worse when you have to continually see the other person enjoying their blessing right in front of your face. Talk about a dagger through the heart!

Hannah of the Bible felt exactly this way as she pleaded with God to give her a baby. Yet year after year her womb remained closed by the Lord and she watched her husband's other wife give birth to multiple children. Adding insult to injury, the Bible also says that the other wife kept "provoking her to irritate her" to the point that Hannah refused to eat.

Then finally, Hannah prayed through her bitter tears and the Lord answered her with a son. She named him Samuel because she said, "I requested him of the Lord." The birth of Samuel prompted her to sing this song:

I'm walking on air. I'm laughing at my rivals. I'm dancing my salvation (I Samuel 2:1 The Message).

But the truly interesting fact about this story is that Hannah didn't keep Samuel for her own. In fact, the word *requested* in Samuel's name means "to borrow." Hannah knew that Samuel ultimately belonged to the Lord and she would only be borrowing him for a short time. Yet how wonderful it felt to have the desires of her heart met by the only One who could give her what she requested of Him!

If you are in the hard season of waiting, take heart and keep praying. He hears you. However, when the Lord gives you what you have asked of Him, sing your song. The wise woman knows that her blessing ultimately belongs to Him, even as she is walking on air!

LORD, YOU ARE OUR TRUE REASON FOR WALKING ON AIR. THANK YOU FOR HEARING OUR PRAYERS.

JESUS IS THE LIGHT

Her daughter sat at the kitchen counter while she was cooking dinner and exclaimed, "Mom, did you know that the sun and moon were created on the fourth day?"

She made a huffing noise and said, "No, honey. Light was created on the first day. Look it up."

"I did, Mom, and it says that *light* was created on the first day but the sun and moon didn't show up until later. Isn't that cool?"

She put her spoon down and risked burning dinner to see if what her daughter was saying was true. She quickly flipped to Genesis 1 and, lo and behold, it was true!

The creation of the seas, trees, vegetation, etc., occurred *before* the sun or moon showed up! How could that be? God explains why in the Gospel of John:

> *In the beginning was the Word, and the Word was with God, and the Word was God. He was with God in the beginning. Through Him all things were made; without Him nothing was made that has been made (John 1:1–3 NIV).*

Jesus is the light and Jesus was there at creation. There is no life for mankind without the light! There is no light without the life of Jesus! The sheer fact that we have life running through our bodies testifies that light has entered the world.

When we begin to view Jesus as our Creator and our life-sustainer, it becomes a game changer for us. Our relationship with Him is not just optional, it is necessary as our source of life. It's then that we understand that the light inside us comes from our salvation in Jesus Christ. Without Him, there is no light to shine.

Friend, have you allowed His light to come into your life? You were created with a purpose, and Jesus would love nothing more than for you to give your life to Him. Today is a great day to start shining!

JESUS, THANK YOU FOR YOUR LIFE-GIVING LIGHT. JUST LIKE THE MOON REFLECTS THE SUN, WE WANT TO REFLECT YOUR LIGHT.

YOU MUST SHINE
AMONG THEM LIKE
STARS LIGHTING UP
THE SKY, AS YOU
OFFER THEM THE
MESSAGE OF LIFE.

PHILIPPIANS 2:15–16 GNT

MORE THAN ENOUGH GRACE

Grief is a paradox of sorts. It can bring us to our knees in an instant, yet if properly walked through, it can be the thing that brings us closer to God than ever before.

The moment that she found out that her little brother had been killed in a car accident, her life changed. She thought to herself that her life would never again be the same, and she was right. It would never be the same. But it wouldn't always be as terrible as it was in that moment.

As the days turned into weeks that turned into months, she began to experience the various stages of grief: denial, anger, bargaining, depression, and acceptance. The happy-go-lucky conversations with God turned into full-on boxing matches with the one she called Father.

Noooo! I don't believe it. I won't believe it.

How could You? You call Yourself good?

I'll do anything. Just let him rise like You did for Martha and Mary when You resurrected their brother Lazarus.

Where are You in all of this? Don't You love me?

These real and raw conversations scared her. She was afraid that she would lose her faith in the One who had the power to get her through this awful time. That is until she heard Him whisper these words to her broken heart,

My grace is always more than enough for you,
My daughter. You don't need to worry because
I am not astonished by your weakness. In fact,
My power finds its full expression through your
weakness. So bring it on. Bring all of your weakness
to Me (paraphrase of II Corinthians 12:9).

Oh, how her aching soul needed to hear those words. He was not astonished by her words of brokenness, but rather, He lavished His grace on her in that moment. Grace that was more than enough.

FATHER, TEACH US TO COME TO YOU WITH
OUR BROKENNESS AND RECEIVE THE
GRACE THAT ONLY YOU CAN GIVE.

NO EQUAL

Remember the old cartoons where the character had a devil and his pitchfork on one shoulder and an angel on the other? The character is seemingly caught in the middle of a heated debate, his head whipping from left to right and back again. The devil is typically more persuasive and leads the character into temptation, and the angel becomes an afterthought, no match for the little devil. It's all fun and games and eventually the character sees the devil for who he truly is, yet conveniently leaves all the damage that has been done in the meantime for someone else to clean up.

Unfortunately, we don't have the same luxury in our everyday lives. When we choose the path of temptation, there are usually very real and painful consequences that follow. But what we need to remember is that we serve a God who is bigger than the devil. They are certainly not equals, even though the world depicts them as so.

According to Scripture, the devil is *our* enemy and he seeks to devour us and our families, but he is no match for the Almighty. John reminds us that we belong to God and because we do, His Spirit defends us. We need not worry because God is greater than the devil could ever think of being. And as a bonus, if we know God's Word then we know how this story ends: with the enemy defeated once and for all.

In I John 4:4 NCV, we read,

My dear children, you belong to God and have defeated them; because God's Spirit, who is in you, is greater than the devil, who is in the world.

So, when the devil comes to deceive us, as he undoubtedly will, we are wise to call upon the name of the One who is greater than the one who is in the world. His name is Jesus!

ALMIGHTY GOD, WE BELIEVE THAT YOU ARE GREATER THAN THE ENEMY WHO COMES TO DEVOUR US, AND WE CALL UPON THE NAME OF JESUS TO DEFEND US. YOU HAVE NO EQUAL.

ALL GOOD

It was the activity that her children had most been looking forward to while in the mountains: the zip line adventure park. After the instructor took his time to teach them how to twizzle between obstacle courses, he checked their gear for safety one last time and said, "You guys have fun out there!"

"Wait, what?! You're not coming with us?" she called as he was walking away. "Nope. You're all good." That was not exactly how she saw this thing playing out in her mind.

As she shakily set out on the first tightrope, she determined to keep her eyes up and not on the ground far beneath her. But as her ankles wobbled, so did her confidence. She knew that the ropes would catch her if she fell, but she didn't know how she would recover if she were left dangling in the air for everyone to see. With sweaty palms and every one of her core muscles, she slowly but surely made it to the other side, breathing heavily as she put both feet on the platform. "All good, indeed," she exhaled.

In real life, there will be situations where the Lord calls us to step out in faith. It may be scary, like walking a tightrope in the mountains. Our hearts may be beating out of our chests, but if we lay all our fears before Him and trust Him to catch us if we fall, then we can use our core muscles, and before we know it, we've made it to the other side.

Trusting God doesn't mean that all fear goes way. It means that we do what God has called us to do in spite of our fear because we have full confidence in His ability to save us, just like David did when he said,

But in the day that I'm afraid, I lay all my fears before You and trust in You with all my heart (Psalm 56:3 TPT).

That's when we can exhale and truly feel as if everything is "all good."

GOD, WE TRUST YOU WITH ALL OUR HEARTS.
WE ASK THAT YOU HELP US TO STEP OUT
IN CONFIDENCE DESPITE OUR FEARS.

LIGHT IS SWEET

There is just something about a beautiful day filled with sunshine, isn't there? Especially after multiple days of cold weather. When the weather is dull and dreary, it's not long before even the optimist's bones cry out for the warmth that only the sun can provide.

King Solomon said it best in Ecclesiastes 11:7 NIV:

Light is sweet, and it pleases the eyes to see the sun.

But what if you're not feeling the sun and its warmth right now? What if you're in a season of your life where all you feel is the bitter chill and the darkness settling in your heart? You are not alone. In fact, Solomon understood how this felt.

In the very next verse he says to "remember the days of darkness for there will be many." That's the thing about life. Try as we might, we cannot have only days filled with sunshine. That's why we need a Savior who understands what this feels like. He's gone through the same days of darkness. The book of Hebrews tells us that He experienced every human emotion—all the pain, all the testing—and would be able to help where help was needed (Hebrews 2:18). It's as if He says to us, "I know what it feels like to be alone, betrayed, abandoned, depressed. I've experienced every one of these emotions and I get you. You are not alone."

Because Jesus experienced what we experience on earth, He is truly able to bring us the help we need and the sweetest of light into our darkest day.

So then, we are wise to enjoy the days of sunshine when they come and reach to the light when they're dark. Light is indeed sweet.

JESUS, WE ASK YOU TO BRING YOUR SWEET LIGHT
INTO OUR DARK DAYS AND GIVE US WISDOM
TO ENJOY THE ONES FILLED WITH SUNSHINE.

THE WHOLE TRUTH

Sometimes it really is hard to tell the truth. Even for adults.

If you have spent any amount of time parenting littles, then you probably have tried your best to teach them to "always tell the truth." Mothers can usually tell if their sweet angels are not being truthful by the way they act if they've been asked a direct question. But if there's a situation where the mother didn't know to ask them a question and the truth is conveniently omitted—well, that's the same thing as telling a lie. This is a tricky one for their little minds because "technically" they didn't tell an outright lie, but it doesn't change the fact that the whole truth was not presented.

This same principle can be applied to us as adults. In a world where the truth is becoming more and more gray, what is your truth is not necessarily mine and vice versa. And that's exactly why we absolutely must go back to the original source of truth.

In John 17:17 NIV, Jesus prays for His disciples this specific prayer:

Sanctify them by the truth; Your word is truth.

The word *sanctify* means to live a set-apart lifestyle. It's a life that looks different than the world. And the only way that we are going to do that is if we have the Spirit of Jesus living inside of us and we know His Word! His Word is the ultimate truth and it holds all the answers we need to live a set-apart life.

It's not always easy to go against mainstream society, but if we are going to present the whole truth, then we must say that Jesus is Lord and stand on His Word.

FATHER, WE PRAY TO YOU JUST AS YOUR SON JESUS DID. SET US APART FROM THE WORLD BY THE TRUTH. WE BELIEVE YOUR WORD IS TRUTH.

THE ROAD TO FREEDOM

Have you ever been in a darkness so thick you could physically feel the weight of it? You desperately wanted to be free of the darkness, but you couldn't seem to shake it loose.

This is such a heavy place to be. Sometimes we find ourselves in the darkness through no fault of our own. It could be that we are grieving the loss of a loved one or are in physical pain.

But oftentimes we live in darkness due to a sin that we have allowed to come into our lives, such as addiction, lust, pride, or even laziness. As we fall deeper and deeper into the trap, we begin to feel the chains bind us and we are helpless to escape.

Yet God never intended for us to live this way, so He provided a way out when He sent His Son, Jesus, to die for our sins. When we accept Jesus' free gift of salvation, His light is put inside us and it is the catalyst to our freedom.

Psalm 107:14 (TPT) says,

His light broke through the darkness and He led us out in freedom from death's dark shadow and snapped every one of our chains.

When His light enters, darkness has no choice but to flee. Walking in the light is not a cakewalk, but it is the road to freedom. It takes intentionality and faith. Yet as we take a step toward it, then another, and then another, we feel those chains start to snap, and before we know it, we are running full steam ahead in complete freedom. That is how the light breaks through the darkness.

GOD, SOMETIMES THE DARKNESS IS SO THICK
WE CAN'T SEE THE ROAD TO FREEDOM. WE NEED
YOUR LIGHT TO COME INTO OUR SITUATION AND
HELP US. WE'RE SO SORRY TO HAVE DISAPPOINTED
YOU IN ANY WAY. HELP US TO TRUST YOU WITH
EVERYTHING. GIVE US THE FAITH TO WALK
IN THE LIGHT. SNAP OUR CHAINS, LORD!

EVEN IF

Sometimes we're walking through life and it all makes total sense. And then there are times when absolutely nothing makes sense. Perhaps we were simply minding our own business, but suddenly our legs were kicked out from under us, leaving us wondering what in the world just happened.

Surely Martha and Mary felt somewhat similar when all of a sudden their beloved brother became sick with a life-threatening illness that required immediate attention. They did some quick thinking and sent word to their friend Jesus and asked Him to come on the double!

Jesus received the message and responded in a curious way,

Now Jesus loved Martha and her sister and Lazarus. So when He heard that Lazarus was sick, He stayed where He was two more days (John 11:5–6 NIV).

Wait. What? One of His very best friends was sick, so He stayed put?

By the time Jesus got there four days later Lazarus was dead, and Martha let Him know her displeasure. "Where have You been? If You had been here, he would not be dead!"

Adding to His mysterious behavior, Jesus replied in the most cryptic way. "I am the resurrection and the life. The one who believes in Me will live, even though they die; and whoever lives by believing in Me will never die. Do you believe this?" (John 11:25–26 NIV).

To say that we believe when life is good doesn't take much faith. But we have to be willing to ask ourselves this question when life throws us that inevitable curveball.

Because believing Jesus is the truth is easy enough UNTIL...

your brother dies;
you miscarry that baby that you waited and prayed for;
your spouse confesses the unthinkable to you;

...THEN it's personal.
But faith is believing EVEN IF...

your brother stays in the grave;
your arms remain empty;
your spouse refuses to come home;

...trusting in His supreme plan.

JESUS, WE BELIEVE IN YOU AND YOUR PLANS
FOR US. HELP US TO TRUST YOU EVEN IF...

WORDS AS SWEET AS HONEY

The school children squealed with delight as they entered the gates of the local zoo on their highly anticipated field trip. It was a beautiful day with weather just right for the animals to show off their tricks…monkeys swinging through the air spurred on by applause and a cute baby hippo performing to receive food. So when the kids came across the foxes' den they were ready to see what these animals could do.

There were two foxes in the cage but only one had been given a boiled egg. As you can imagine, the fox who had been left out was not too happy and began chasing the fox with the egg. She ran him up and over logs at a rapid pace until she cornered him and began aggressively biting him. The little boys in the group were shouting, "Whoa! Look at them fight!" as the little girls clutched their mamas and teachers. The foxes continued their quest for dominance while the group walked away a little disturbed.

This scenario is reminiscent of Paul's warning in Galatians 5:15 (NIV):

If you bite and devour each other, watch out
or you will be destroyed by each other.

Ouch. Are we jealously biting our sisters or brothers

with our words, trying to take away from them a blessing that they have received? Or are we just petty and careless with our words? Regardless of motivation, bite marks are inevitably being left on that person.

Conversely, the Bible says that "gracious words are a honeycomb, sweet to the soul and healing to the bones" (Proverbs 16:24 NIV). When we use our words to lift others up, then we not only feed their soul, but we also act as a healing balm. Now that's a trick worth cheering for!

O LORD, LET OUR WORDS BE AS SWEET AS
HONEY. LET THEM BE USED TO BRING HEALING
TO OUR FRIENDS AND FAMILY RATHER THAN
LEAVE NASTY BITE MARKS ON THEM.

RESPOND TO HIS FAVOR

Grace. The word carries such beauty, yet it can slip through our fingers like the seeds of a dandelion when blown free in the wind. We want to grab hold of it, but oftentimes its ethereal connotation leaves us wondering what grace really is.

Grace is "showing favor" or giving someone "a gracious gift" of more than they deserve. It's like coming home from work to find your house completely spotless, yet knowing that when you left in the morning it was a wreck…dishes in the sink, beds unmade, dog paw prints all over the floor. When you walked in the door, it not only looked amazing, but it smelled great too. You didn't hire anyone to clean for you; it was just a gracious gift given to you. You have received favor.

When Jesus came to give you salvation, it was a gracious gift extended just because He loves you. Nothing you could ever do would merit such an extravagant gift. In fact, when He came for you, your heart was a wreck…it was dirty and foul, filled with selfish desires. But because of His great favor, you have been made clean and filled with light.

In II Corinthians 6:1–2 (TPT), we read,

We beg you not to take God's marvelous grace for granted, allowing it to have no effect on

your lives…. Now is the time to respond to
His favor! Now is the day of salvation!

God's marvelous grace is not to be taken for granted. If we have received His gift of salvation, it should change every part of our lives. We don't look like the same women we used to be because we have been radically changed. When people see our lives, they are able to tell that we have been granted a deep-seated joy.

If you have not accepted God's free gift of grace, you can do it today! He loves you beyond all comprehension and He's ready to pour out His blessings on you. Will you accept His gift and give Him all your worries, fears, concerns, and problems and let Him fill your life with peace? Now is the time!

O LORD, HOW AMAZING IT IS TO BE
SHOWN SUCH LOVE. MAY WE NEVER GET
OVER YOUR MARVELOUS GRACE!

DON'T SHINE
SO OTHERS CAN
SEE YOU. SHINE
SO THAT THROUGH
YOU, OTHERS
CAN SEE HIM.

C.S. Lewis

BE YOURSELF

Do you ever find it hard to be confident in yourself? You deeply desire to be that person with her head held high, but insecurity starts creeping in and before you know it, you're shrinking back into your shell. Why? Do you feel too old, too young, too fat, too skinny, too scared of what others will think of you? You're not alone, dear one.

However, insecurity is one of the tactics used by the enemy to keep us from being effective in Kingdom work while here on earth. He knows that if he can make us think that our efforts aren't "good enough" or that we aren't as pretty/gifted/admired as our sister, then we automatically disqualify ourselves before anyone has a chance to see what gifts we do have to offer.

The apostle Paul knew that Timothy needed to hear some words of encouragement in this area, so he wrote to him,

Don't let anyone put you down because you're young.
Teach believers with your life: by word, by demeanor, by
love, by faith, by integrity (I Timothy 4:12 The Message).

You don't have to be anyone other than you. It doesn't matter how old or young you are, what your waist size or your IQ is, or even how much Scripture you know. You have something to contribute to this world, and it desperately needs your light! So live YOUR life so that it points others to Christ: encouraging others with your words, exhibiting a kind demeanor, loving others well, living out your faith, having great integrity. That's how you beat the insecurity and shine with all your beautiful being! Be yourself.

O LORD, YOU KNOW HOW THE ENEMY LOVES
TO MAKE US FEEL INSECURE AND RENDER US
INEFFECTIVE FOR YOUR KINGDOM. TEACH US
HOW TO BE COMFORTABLE BEING WHO YOU
HAVE CALLED US TO BE. MAKE US SHINE!

NO RAIN, NO RAINBOW

Dolly Parton once said, "The way I see it, if you want the rainbow, you gotta put up with the rain."

The very first rainbow was seen by Noah and his family after the great flood, and it became a symbol of God's covenant to never flood the earth again (see Genesis 9:8–17). A rainbow is also mentioned when Ezekiel had a vision of the glory of the Lord. He recorded,

There was a brilliant light all around Him. The appearance of the brilliant light all around was like that of a rainbow in a cloud on a rainy day. This was the appearance of the form of the LORD's glory (Ezekiel 1:27–28 HCSB).

But what if Ezekiel had never been through a rainy day? What if his days were only filled with copious amounts of sunshine and no dark clouds ever graced the sky? Would the light have shown up so brilliantly if it were not contrasted against a cloudy, rainy day? Probably not.

The same is true for us, friend. Do you think that if we only lived a life filled with sweet times and memories we would be able to recognize them for how sweet they truly are? Would the light of Christ shine as brightly through us if we never had to go through hard times? Probably not.

Dark days are a natural part of life, but if we allow the light to shine through, then we get the rainbows. Dolly had it right after all. What's a little rain when the outcome is the beauty of reflecting light?

FATHER GOD, WE WANT TO SEE YOUR GLORY
AND IF THAT MEANS THAT WE HAVE TO PUT UP
WITH THE RAINY DAYS, THEN SO BE IT. MAY
EACH ONE TEACH US TO REFLECT YOUR LIGHT.

STAYING IN THE POCKET

Ever since he was a young child, he had been an excellent drummer, which he considered a true gift and a means to glorify God through worship. While playing on the university drum line in college he learned an important concept in music that he referred to as "staying in the pocket."

Because the drummer leads the rhythm of the song, it is important that he doesn't play ahead of the beat or behind it but rather right in the pocket. And when he does, the other musicians can follow the pocket of rhythm and it becomes the natural resting place, making the song flow perfectly. But imagine if the drummer is playing his beat but the bass player starts doing his own thing to a different tempo. It won't be long before the vocalist is confused and the song is completely off track.

Staying in the pocket is vital if we want to create the very best music possible.

This is an important concept for us to learn in our everyday lives as well. If we want this life of ours to flow naturally, we have to learn how to follow the lead of the Spirit and not get ahead of Him yet not lag too far behind either. We have to stay in His perfect pocket and resist the temptation to start marching to the beat of our own drum.

David spoke of this exact thing when he said in Psalm 108:1 (NIV),

> *My heart, O God, is steadfast; I will sing*
> *and make music with all my soul.*

Just like David did, we can keep our hearts in beat with the Spirit, ensuring that we are following His lead, not our own. That is how He will be most glorified in our lives, resulting in the most beautiful music to our King.

HOLY SPIRIT, WE WANT NOTHING MORE THAN TO
BE LED BY YOU, STAYING IN THE POCKET, LETTING
OUR SOUL FLOW PERFECTLY WITH YOURS.

ALWAYS BE READY

I f someone asked you, "What is the gospel?" do you feel as if you could give a good answer?

Sometimes Christian words such as *grace, salvation,* and *gospel* are so familiar to us that we lose the significance of their meaning, or we never had a good working definition of them rooted in our mind.

I Peter 3:15 NLT tells us,

> *If someone asks about your hope as a believer, always be ready to explain it.*

But how can we effectively communicate the hope that we have as Christ followers if we're not exactly sure what it is that we believe?

The answer lies in the fact that we must always go back to the Word as our ultimate source of truth. It's as simple as opening our Bible app and typing in the word *gospel.* When we do, we find this beautiful word actually means "good news!" And the good news is that Jesus, the Son of God, came to earth so that He could die for our sins (which is *salvation*), even though we didn't deserve it (which is *grace*) and that He didn't stay dead, but that He was resurrected and is coming back again (which is our *hope* as a believer!)

Now that is good news! And it's all there for the taking if we are willing to dig around a little bit. Don't be intimidated by the big "Christian words." Simply open God's Word consistently and stand amazed as the good news starts to change your ordinary life into a life that shines for Him.

Before you know it, you'll be more than ready to share the hope that He has given you, and that's truly good news!

LORD, GIVE US THE CONFIDENCE TO ALWAYS BE
READY TO SHARE OUR FAITH WITH OTHERS.
WE HAVE THE MOST AWESOME HOPE AS
BELIEVERS, AND WE WANT TO BE ABLE TO
EXPLAIN THE GOOD NEWS TO OTHERS.

GOOD EYES

On a scale of one to ten, how often do you think about money? Not the normal thoughts of providing for your family in order to live a comfortable lifestyle but rather allowing the pursuit of money to dictate your motives, friendships, and conversations. It's not uncommon for money to be a driving force in our lives. And while money itself is not bad or evil, it can skew our vision and our hearts if we're not careful.

Jesus had much to say on the topic of money. He told His followers that they should not put their trust in material wealth because eventually it would rot and decay just like everything else. Instead, we are wise to put our trust in God, who is eternal. In order to get His point across, He said in Matthew 6:22 (NIV),

The eye is the lamp of the body. If your eyes are healthy, your whole body will be full of light.

Our eyes are what illuminate our entire being. And if our eyes are good, meaning that if we fill our eyes with eternally focused things (like the gospel)—rather than lusting after the material things that the world tells us are important—then our whole being will be filled with light.

On the flip side, if we try to fill our lives up with worldly treasures, then our body is full of darkness. How many know this to be true? It doesn't take more than a brief glance through a celebrity-centered magazine to know that a life focused on worldly passions and money is not soul-satisfying in the least.

The eyes are the lamp of our bodies. We get to choose if we want to fill them with light or darkness. Money is vital to our everyday lives, but we get to say if it controls us or vice versa. Good eyes know the difference and they are illuminated by the light.

JESUS, WE WANT OUR WHOLE LIVES TO BE A REFLECTION OF YOUR LIGHT. TRAIN OUR EYES TO BE FILLED WITH YOU RATHER THAN MATERIAL WEALTH.

MUSCLE MEMORY

Every Tuesday and Thursday the same exercise class was offered at the local gym for strength training. The class was typically filled with the same faithful members who knew the routine by heart. They assembled their individual workstations and greeted each other as they stretched and waited to begin. However, one particular morning the instructor could not be there to teach the class in person, so they were to follow a prerecorded video. The only glitch was that the audio was coming through the technology but the video screen remained completely dark.

However, the members did not throw down their towels and storm out the door. Instead, they all instinctively perked up their ears and picked up their bars. They simultaneously started exercising both their muscles and their memory! Lift for two, down for two.

There's a spiritual principle to be learned here. Sometimes we feel as if we are surrounded by pitch-black darkness, but if we perk up our ears to listen to the Holy Spirit's voice we can follow His direction back into the light.

I John 2:8 NLT assures us that,

The darkness is disappearing,
and the true light is already shining.

The disciple John knew what it felt like to be enveloped in the darkness after he witnessed Jesus die a horrific death on the cross. But he also saw with his own eyes the resurrection of Jesus and testified to the return of the light! Yet he had to rely on his muscle memory to get him through those three dark days.

That's a promise we can hold onto whenever we feel as if we are in darkness. We only need to let our muscle memory take over a few steps at a time until we can see clearly once again the true light that is already shining!

JESUS, SOMETIMES OUR VISION GETS BLOCKED
AND THE DARK DAYS ENVELOP US. ENCOURAGE US
TO EXERCISE OUR MUSCLE MEMORY KNOWING
THAT THE LIGHT IS ALREADY SHINING.

YOUR LANTERN AND COMPASS

It's not hard to lose our sense of direction in this big world. Even the smartest of adventurers have to pull out their GPS to make sure that they are still on track. If not, things can go sideways in a hurry.

Expert hikers know that first you need to decide where it is that you want to end up. Your final destination is the goal that you are reaching toward, and typically it is worth the physical effort. Before you set out, you'll want to study the map and make sure that you have your flashlight packed as well as a compass so that you don't end up walking in circles. In fact, as you stop periodically for water breaks it's important to pull that compass out and check yourself. True north never lies and will keep you on track to your destination. As night falls, your flashlight will guide your feet along the path to safety, getting you one step closer to your destination.

All these tools were seen as valuable to the psalmist as he set out to reach his ultimate destination, the sacred mountain of the Lord. In Psalm 43:3 (The Message), we read,

*Give me Your lantern and compass, give me
a map, so I can find my way to the sacred
mountain, to the place of Your presence.*

Before he set out on his hike, he knew that he needed a lantern, a compass, and a map. But notice that he asks that the Lord give him "*Your* lantern and compass." These weren't the regular accessories you can buy at the local sporting goods store. These were tools given to him by the Lord. The lantern would light his way upon the path when the darkness came, and the compass would steer his feet in the right direction according to true north.

Such tools are also available to us in our spiritual life. God graciously gives us the light and truth of His Word to guide us to the most wonderful of places, His presence.

GOD, WE WANT YOUR LANTERN AND YOUR COMPASS
TO GUIDE US AS WE WALK THROUGH THIS LIFE.
KEEP US ON YOUR PATH AND IN YOUR PRESENCE.

REAL REFLECTIONS

Do you ever look in the mirror and wonder whose reflection is staring back at you? You hardly recognize the person whom you have become. The mirror isn't lying to you. It's just that your reflection doesn't resemble what you look like in your head.

In your mind you've got it all together. You're crushing it as a mom. You've been consistently speaking your husband's love language. Your boss is surely going to give you that promotion any day now. The house is clean…well, let's not go that far. But really, all in all you've got a pretty good beat on things.

So why is this reflection making you feel like a fraud? Is there something deeper that needs to be dealt with?

Proverbs 27:19 (NLT) says,

As a face is reflected in water, so the
heart reflects the real person.

If you have chosen to follow Jesus, then His very Spirit dwells inside your heart and can help you discern whether you are a fraud or not. Are you presenting yourself as something you are not (i.e., totally unselfish in relationships, the martyr mom, a saint in the workplace)? If so, then it's probably time to check back into God's Word and see what He has to say on topics such as pride, humility, and sin. But it could be that the reason your reflection seems off is that the enemy is distorting it by telling you that you're not good enough, you need to work to gain love, and that God is disappointed in you. All are lies and should be counteracted with God's Word.

If our hearts reflect who we really are, then it makes sense to fill them with God's declarations of love and mercy. That's how we stop feeling like a fraud and reflect our true heart.

O LORD, GIVE US YOUR WORDS TO FILL OUR
HEARTS WITH. WE WANT OUR REFLECTIONS
TO BE FILLED WITH LOVE AND LIGHT.

THE BEST DEFENSE

Do you ever stop to ponder what you're prone to put your faith in? Is it your spouse, your retirement accounts, or perhaps your good looks?

There is the obvious "Christian answer": of course we put our faith in Jesus. But when the rubber meets the road, is this really true? When my child makes a poor decision that has public repercussions, where is my faith? Or when my investments lose value and I have to drastically cut my living expenses, where is my faith? When I face bone-crushing rejection, where is my faith?

These are the kind of real-life experiences that give us pause and make us reevaluate exactly where we are placing our faith.

Ephesians 6:16 HCSB says,

> *In every situation take the shield of faith,*
> *and with it you will be able to extinguish*
> *all the flaming arrows of the evil one.*

Did you notice how this verse said that we are to take up the shield of faith in *every* situation? Not just the situations where it's easy to keep the faith, but in every. single. one.

Paul also wants us to realize that placing our faith in

Christ alone is the only way that we are going to fight off the flaming arrows of the enemy, which come hot and fast. If we keep putting our faith in the wrong places (e.g., our loved ones, money, or physical appearances) then we will be disappointed when they inevitably fail us. Doing so also leaves us exposed to the enemy's attacks. But when we trust God to defend us, then we can fend off the enemy and our faith is strengthened!

So, what are we waiting for? Let's pick up that shield and put our faith where it belongs. After all, He is our best defense.

JESUS, OUR FAITH IS IN YOU ALONE. GIVE US EYES TO SEE THE ATTACKS OF THE ENEMY. STRENGTHEN OUR FAITH IN YOU AS WE TAKE UP OUR SHIELD.

BUT IF MY FIRE IS
NOT LARGE IT IS YET
REAL, AND THERE MAY
BE THOSE WHO CAN
LIGHT THEIR CANDLE
AT ITS FLAME.

A.W. TOZER, *THE PURSUIT OF GOD*

AWESOME POWER

The hand of God is a mighty thing. It can move mountains. It can calm the stormy seas. It can strike humankind down. It can heal the blind. It can cause dread as well as silence fears. It can feed you, clothe you, and protect you. It can give and take away. It can form a human from dust. And it can raise the dead to life.

It is not possible to fully comprehend the hand of God, but it is appropriate to stand in awe of its awesome power.

The Old Testament prophet Habakkuk saw God moving across the deserts and said that His coming was as brilliant as the sunrise. Rays of light were flashing from His hands where His awesome power was hidden. What a scene Habakkuk was privy to! He was able to not only witness the brilliance of the Almighty but also see exactly how His hands work.

How amazing to know that the source of His limitless power is accompanied by light! The very same light that He puts inside those of us who believe in Him. Could this mean that we have access to His awesome power as well?

Jesus said in Acts 1:8 (HCSB),

You will receive power when the Holy Spirit has come on you.

The word for power is *dynamis*, meaning "the ability to perform a mighty deed by God's supernatural power." It's a power like no other, and you, my friend, have access to it!

The reason Jesus wants us to have this awesome power is so that we will be witnesses about Him everywhere we go as a light for the nations. And to think, it was His light-flashing hand that formed us in the first place. Oh, to behold the awesome hand of the Lord!

GOD, THERE ARE NO WORDS TO DESCRIBE THE
AWESOMENESS OF YOUR HAND. WE STAND IN
AWE AND THANK YOU FOR FORMING US IN
YOUR MAGNIFICENT LIGHT AND POWER.

EMBRACING CHANGE

Few things spark both excitement and discomfort like change, yet the fact remains that change is inevitable.

It's not always easy to embrace the big changes in life, such as a child moving off to start college or transitioning into a new job or, perhaps, coming to the realization that your aging parent needs more care than you can provide. Change can bring feelings of sadness or anxiety as we attempt to chart these new waters.

However, not all change is bad. There can be the change of family dynamics when a new foster child comes to live with you, or the change of address when you finally move into your new home.

Whatever the circumstance, change brings with it the chance for a new beginning, a metamorphosis, just as a caterpillar changes into a butterfly...that is, *if* the change is embraced.

Paul wrote in Colossians 1:6 NLT,

This same Good News that came to you is going out all over the world. It is bearing fruit everywhere by changing lives, just as it changed your lives from the day you first heard and understood the truth about God's wonderful grace.

Think about how the gospel has changed your life. Accepting Christ requires a lifestyle change, meaning that we have to let go of some of the things that once brought us comfort. However, once the old things pass away, we begin to see a newness take over our lives. Just as the butterfly realizes she was never meant to stay in that cocoon, we too can let go of the familiar and press on to a new creation. To live inside His wonderful grace is worth any and all transitions that have to happen. It's a change worth embracing!

GOD, WE DESIRE TO BE CHANGED BY
THE GOSPEL MORE THAN WE DESIRE TO
STAY IN OUR OLD PATTERNS. CHANGE US
WITH YOUR WONDERFUL GRACE.

TREASURED POSSESSION

She wasn't exactly sure how it happened, but somehow a brand-new white sofa now sat in her home.

It was so beautiful and comfy in the showroom and contrasted perfectly with the charcoal paint that adorned the walls. But what she hadn't accounted for was her eleven- and nine-year-old children who also lived in the house and how their grimy little hands and feet would surely find their way onto the white couch. "Not to worry," the saleswoman said, "it has performance fabric and should be fine."

But, of course, she couldn't help being that crazy mom, constantly telling them things like, *Take your shoes off before you sit down. Are your hands clean? Remember I said no nacho cheese on the couch!* She found herself repeatedly wiping off the dirt trails they left behind, trying desperately to preserve her treasured possession.

In the Bible, God calls His people His treasured possession. This specific phrase indicates a desire to preserve the special treasure because of the extreme value that it holds for the owner.

That, my friend, is how God perceives us. As something so valuable that He will do whatever it takes to preserve us as His special treasure. He loved and cherished us enough to sacrifice His Son so that we can be included as His chosen people.

In Deuteronomy 14:2 (NIV) we read,

For you are a people holy to the LORD your God. Out of all the peoples on the face of the earth, the LORD has chosen you to be His treasured possession.

And when we get dirty and stained, the Father lovingly comes behind us and wipes us clean so that we are once again white as snow. We don't deserve it, but oh how special it feels to be so treasured, gleaming for all the world to see.

FATHER, THANK YOU FOR CHERISHING US AS YOUR
TREASURED POSSESSION AND FOR CLEANSING
US FROM OUR SIN TIME AND TIME AGAIN.
PRESERVE US SO THAT WE CAN SHINE FOR YOU.

POWER THROUGH

She rubbed her temples and thought, *Lord, I don't have time for this. Make the throbbing go away, please.*

The headaches always seemed to come on at the most inconvenient times. When there was a work deadline to meet or while attending one of her daughter's basketball games. No amount of ibuprofen could compete with a sounding buzzer. Pressure plus pain equaled down for the count.

These bodies of ours are prone to ailments from time to time. Fevers, headaches, and even infection can slow us down from our productivity, putting us in bed when we need to be up and going.

The Gospel of Matthew records a time that Peter's mother-in-law was sick in bed with a fever. When Jesus saw her lying there, He simply touched her hand and the fever left her. But then the truly miraculous happened. Matthew said,

> *Then she got up and began to serve Him (Matthew 8:15 HCSB).*

One minute she's totally out of commission and the next she's up serving again with a supernatural strength that every woman would like to possess.

However, it's interesting to note that Jesus never told her to get up and power through so that she could serve Him. She did that on her own. It seems as if she was so thankful to be out of that bed that she jumped at the chance to serve her Healer. She didn't view her service as an imposition but rather as an act of gratitude, and that's why we know her story today.

We are wise to learn from this woman's example. The next time that we are down for the count and Jesus heals us with the touch of His hand, let's have the wherewithal to power through and continue our service to Him.

JESUS, TOUCH US WITH YOUR HEALING
HAND WHEN OUR BODIES ARE DOWN FOR
THE COUNT. GIVE US STRENGTH TO GET UP
SO THAT WE MAY SERVE YOU BETTER.

PRAYER POSSE

They call themselves the Prayer Posse and they take it seriously. Oh sure, there are the funny memes that get passed around via text, but for the most part they are there to encourage and pray for each other as well as anyone within their circles. After almost ten years of daily contact the variety of prayer requests is vast, ranging from potty-training children to house building to losing loved ones. They've seen each other through master's degrees, health scares, job changes, and sleepless nights. Where one leaves off in a sentence, the next can finish it, and when they ask for prayer, they know the others will truly start praying. Their friendship is a gift from the Lord, and they don't take it for granted.

Daniel of the Old Testament knew the power of praying friends. When King Nebuchadnezzar threatened to kill all the wise men in his kingdom if they couldn't interpret his dream, Daniel wasted no time in asking his companions Hananiah, Mishael, and Azariah to pray to the God of heaven for mercy.

In fact, in Daniel 2:17–18 (The Message) we read,

Daniel then went home and told his companions Hananiah, Mishael, and Azariah what was going on. He asked them to pray to the God of

*heaven for mercy in solving this mystery so that
the four of them wouldn't be killed along with
the whole company of Babylonian wise men.*

As they were praying, the Lord answered them and revealed the mystery to Daniel, and the men's lives were spared.

Daniel knew that he could count on his friends to pray with him. They wouldn't just *say* that they would be praying, but they actually would pray. They had each other's backs and didn't stop until the mystery was revealed. They were the ultimate prayer posse.

Do you have praying friends in your life? If not, consider praying about who God wants to connect you with. He loves a good prayer posse and you will too!

FATHER, THANK YOU FOR THE GIFT OF PRAYING
FRIENDS. LET US NOT ONLY ENCOURAGE
EACH OTHER IN OUR EVERYDAY LIVES BUT
ALSO LET US BE DILIGENT TO PRAY.

FAITHFUL IN PRAYER

She hung up the phone with a bewildered look. She wasn't expecting *that*.

She had gone in for her annual mammogram, but instead of getting the usual "no findings; see you next year" results, she was instructed to have a biopsy on a cyst in her breast. Her mother was a breast cancer survivor so she knew the protocol. As she made arrangements at one of the nation's best cancer institutes, she had complete peace that the test results would come back negative for breast cancer, but because of her family history she wanted to be completely certain that it was nothing.

Her husband added the upcoming appointment to his group prayer list, and before she knew it there was a designated time of prayer set up in her honor. She didn't exactly know how to feel about all this attention, but believing in the power of prayer, she welcomed the opportunity to be lifted up by these friends.

And she was instantly glad that she did! She didn't know how to process it all, but once it was happening she was overcome with gratitude. She could feel their prayers infuse His peace into her just as Scripture says in Philippians 4:6–7 (NIV),

Do not be anxious about anything, but in every
situation, by prayer and petition, with thanksgiving,
present your requests to God. And the peace of God,
which transcends all understanding, will guard
your hearts and your minds in Christ Jesus.

Due to the prayers of her faithful friends, His supernatural peace stayed with her throughout the day of testing. The results of the biopsy were indeed negative, and tears of joy were shed as she shared the good news with her praying friends. They taught her the value of being joyful in hope, patient in affliction, and faithful in prayer.

GOD, THANK YOU FOR THE GIFT OF FAITHFUL
FRIENDS WHO SHED THEIR LIGHT AND LOVE
IN TIMES THAT WE NEED IT THE MOST. LET
US BE WILLING TO BE A FAITHFUL FRIEND FOR
ANOTHER IN THEIR TIME OF AFFLICTION.

HOLD FAST, STAY TRUE

"Do you have what it takes to be an elite achiever?" asked the US Navy SEAL. His consuming presence filled the banquet hall as he enlightened the crowd on how to achieve the most out of their everyday lives.

He pointed to his knuckles where he had tattooed the phrases HOLD FAST and STAY TRUE as a reminder of what to do in the middle of combat. HOLD FAST was so that he could brace himself against the onslaught of his enemies, knowing that they were coming for him hot and fast so he needed to be ready to hold his ground. STAY TRUE helped him remember the principles that he had been taught while training to be a SEAL, knowing that if he deviated from the truth, it could result in death. It also served as a reminder to protect and assist his fellow SEALs in the heat of the battle.

These are life-changing principles for us to live by as well.

I Corinthians 16:13 (NIV) says,

> *Be on your guard; stand firm in the faith; be courageous; be strong.*

In this verse Paul is teaching us the same thing that this navy SEAL was taught in his training. There is an enemy that seeks to kill us. It is imperative that we be on our guard and hold fast against his attacks. Paul also instructs us to stay true to our faith, even when it's hard, even when we're beyond ready to give up, even when we feel lost.

When we know the truth of God's Word, it helps us to see clearly in the heat of the battle, protecting ourselves and our brother and sisters. It's in those moments that the elite achiever takes hold of the light and stays on course.

Be courageous. Be strong. HOLD FAST and STAY TRUE.

LORD, MAKE US STRONG AND COURAGEOUS
THROUGH THE BATTLE. HELP US TO HOLD FAST
TO YOUR WORD AND STAY TRUE IN OUR FAITH.

LIVING YOUR BEST LIFE

She is a miniature labradoodle who loves to run. She's fast and she knows it. Her sense of adventure is off the charts, and if her owner would only let her off her leash, she could totally be living her best life. Sniffing all the smells. Seeing all the sights. But no, she is forced to go only as fast as her owner can walk. Doesn't she know that a dog needs her freedom to run wherever the wind blows? Life on a leash is so unfair.

But what the labradoodle doesn't know is that the owner puts her on a leash because she can see what the small dog can't. Her vision is higher and she can see farther than the dog can with her nose to the ground. In fact, right now she sees a big dog barreling down the driveway ready to attack her dog. But because she's on a leash, the owner can hold her tight and manage the situation. However, if the labradoodle was free to roam, she would most likely be harmed by the dog or oncoming traffic. The owner loves her dog. She knows what is best for her even if the dog can't see it.

God does the same for us in our everyday lives. He knows things that we don't, and His vision is higher than ours.

In Isaiah 55:8–9 (NIV), we read,

"For My thoughts are not your thoughts, neither are

your ways My ways," declares the LORD. *"As the heavens are higher than the earth, so are My ways higher than your ways and My thoughts than your thoughts."*

We tend to think that He is holding us back from living our best life when what He is really doing is protecting us from unforeseen disaster. He keeps us close because He loves us, and once we start to understand His heart, it's then that we truly begin to live our very best life.

FATHER, THANK YOU FOR LOVING US ENOUGH
TO KEEP US CLOSE TO YOU. YOUR WAYS ARE
HIGHER THAN OURS, AND WE SUBMIT TO
YOU IN ORDER TO LIVE OUR BEST LIFE.

PRAISING THROUGH THE PAIN

There are few things that move her to tears on a regular basis; however, worship is one of them. Coming together with other believers and singing of God's faithful love causes grateful tears to spring up inside her.

But there have also been times in her life when the tears have come from a place of pain. After her loved one passed away she would sob uncontrollably as the other voices sang "It Is Well with My Soul." She wondered if she would ever feel like praising again.

But as a faithful Savior so sweetly does, He wrapped His arms around her and began to heal her broken heart. Week by week she returned to worship and eventually she was able to sing again, yet still with hot tears flowing down her cheeks. As the weeks turned into months, the desire to praise her Creator began to return even though she was still grieving. She knew that her hope was in Him.

In Psalm 42:5 (HCSB) the psalmist asks the raw and real questions:

Why am I so depressed? Why this turmoil within me?

But then he answers,

*Put your hope in God, for I will still
praise Him, my Savior and my God.*

Life can create a great state of turmoil, leaving us utterly depressed and believing that we'll never be able to sing praise again. But if we allow ourselves to grieve properly and hold fast to our Savior, before long we'll find that we are able to praise Him even through the pain.

It has been several years since she lost her loved one. The tears still fall from time to time during worship, but they're mostly due to gratitude for all that He's done for her. She will forever put her hope in the One who saved her. He is a faithful God.

GOD, ONLY YOU CAN HEAL A BROKEN HEART.
THANK YOU FOR HOLDING US THROUGH THE
PAIN AND TURMOIL. WE PUT OUR HOPE IN
YOU AND PRAISE YOU FOR WHO YOU ARE.

THE PRIESTLY BLESSING

THE LORD BLESS YOU AND KEEP YOU; THE LORD MAKE HIS FACE SHINE ON YOU AND BE GRACIOUS TO YOU; THE LORD TURN HIS FACE TOWARD YOU AND GIVE YOU PEACE.

Numbers 6:24–26 NIV

FACE-BRIGHTENING WISDOM

Imagine being born of noble birth. You have access to every luxury. Any opportunity or experience you could ever want is right at your fingertips. Yet the one thing that you truly need and desire cannot be bought. It can only be gifted to you. The question is, do you ask for it?

King Solomon was the wisest person to ever live; his fame and proverbs live on to this day. But no amount of money could have bought the wisdom that Solomon possessed. It was a gift from the Lord. I Kings 3 tells of how God told Solomon to ask for whatever he wanted and God would give it to him. Solomon asked for wisdom, claiming to be a little child who did not know how to perform his duties as king. God was so pleased with this that He gave Solomon not only the wisdom he asked for but also wealth and honor! He received *more* than he could have asked or imagined.

We serve a God who is all about giving us more than we can even think to ask Him for, but He truly lights up when we ask Him for wisdom. It gives Him great delight to know that we desire to have the mind of Christ, seeking His wisdom over money or popularity.

Solomon said,

How wonderful to be wise, to analyze and
interpret things. Wisdom lights up a person's face,
softening its harshness. Ecclesiastes 8:1 NLT

No amount of Botox or eye cream can compare to the benefits of godly wisdom. Not only does it soften any harshness in us, but it also transforms every aspect of our lives when we submit to His wisdom. We can analyze and interpret things that would be impossible without God. By allowing the Lord to lead our lives, we are made to shine brighter every single day. The question is, will we be wise enough to ask for such a gift?

GOD, WE ASK YOU FOR WISDOM ABOVE ALL ELSE.
ILLUMINATE OUR LIVES AND FACES WITH IT.

TRAINING TO WIN

Before she could even ask, "How was your day at school, darling?" her daughter handed her a permission slip to compete in the middle school track meet next week.

"A track meet, huh? Are you even physically capable of running a mile without stopping?"

"Psh, Mom, of course I can!"

Knowing the importance of training, she encouraged her daughter by running with her. A few days later they ran another mile just for good measure and called it a good week of training.

When the day of the track meet rolled around, her daughter was pumped and ready to compete. She sat in the stands and cheered wildly when her daughter crossed the finish line, certain that she would be so proud of herself. But instead she found her daughter bent over, complaining that her throat hurt and that her legs were forever ruined. Of course this dramatic reaction was directly correlated to her obvious lack of training. Two practice runs does not make anyone a winning track star.

This same concept applies to our spiritual lives. Hebrews 12:11 NLT says,

No discipline is enjoyable while it is happening—it's painful! But afterward there will be a peaceful harvest of right living for those who are trained in this way.

We cannot open our Bibles every now and then and expect to be spiritually fit. But if we make it a daily discipline to train our minds to be in alignment with His Word, that's when we'll see positive results. It's not easy and can be painful at times as we have to let go of things that are holding us back from running a good race. Yet before long, we're at the finish line holding the victor's crown, because we were training to win.

LORD, KEEP US TRAINING TO WIN EVEN
WHEN IT'S HARD AND PAINFUL. IT'S WORTH
IT TO BE IN ALIGNMENT WITH YOU.

KEEPING GOOD COMPANY

Did your mother ever advise you to pick good friends by reminding you that you are the company you keep? In all her wisdom, she knew that if you chose friends with good moral character, then most likely they would rub off on you. It's a peculiar science that we inevitably become like those we keep company with.

In the book of Acts we see where this timeless advice was heeded by the disciples Peter and John. After healing a disabled man in the name of Jesus, they were locked up by the elders who were none too happy that this miracle.

We read in Acts 4:13 (HCSB),

> *When they observed the boldness of Peter and John and realized that they were uneducated and untrained men, they were amazed and recognized that they had been with Jesus.*

These were ordinary men performing extraordinary wonders to everyone's amazement. How on earth could two fishermen have such boldness and power? The answer is that they had been with Jesus.

Their authentic relationship with Jesus produced a boldness in them that transferred to the way that they ministered to others.

The same boldness is available to us today. There is no prerequisite that we must have a perfect life or multiple degrees in higher education to minister to others. All we need is to follow the example that Peter and John laid out for us.

We must be intentional about being with Jesus, cultivating a relationship through reading His Word and praying. As we do this, our character becomes more and more like the company we keep until finally it is recognizable to the world that we too have been with Jesus.

JESUS, WE WANT PEOPLE TO SEE YOU SHINING OUT OF US. LET US BE WILLING TO KEEP COMPANY WITH YOU DAILY SO THAT IT IS EVIDENT TO THE WORLD THAT WE HAVE BEEN WITH YOU.

CHOOSING TO TRUST

Few things in life are harder to do on a daily basis than to relinquish control. And if your personality thrives on perfectionism, then the struggle is that much more real!

However, the life of a control freak is not all that it's cracked up to be. The minute that inevitable curveball gets thrown our way, we can feel the control starting to slip out of our hands. A medical bill comes in that we can't afford to pay. A family member refuses to reconcile despite our best efforts. A hurricane threatens to dump several inches of rain on our town…again.

Yet if we tune our ears to the voice of the Lord, we hear His words spoken so beautifully through His prophet Isaiah:

You will keep in perfect peace those
whose minds are steadfast, because they
trust in You (Isaiah 26:3 NIV).

Oh, what comfort these words bring. They usher in the ability to release the tight grip of perceived control and allow us to let our minds relax in His perfect peace. Here's the deal: He's in control no matter what. But we can consciously make the choice to give Him our trust or we can be hard headed and do things our own way. The choice is ours to make.

However, the blessing that we find on the other side of that relinquished control is that He gives us perfect peace. It's a peace that only He can provide and it eases our worried minds. Our best attempts at perfectionism do not impress a perfect God; our willingness to trust Him implicitly does.

So when those curveballs hit us out of nowhere, we shake them off because we are choosing to trust the only One who has the ability to keep our minds steadfast and give us perfect peace.

LORD, WE CHOOSE TO GIVE YOU ALL CONTROL AS
WE TRUST YOU IMPLICITLY. KEEP OUR MINDS
STEADFAST AND FILL US WITH YOUR PERFECT PEACE.

WARNING LIGHTS

Oh how she had waited for this day to arrive! In her hand she held a shiny new driver's license and the keys to freedom. She was allowed to drive her father's car, and she was ready to run the roads. However, she had barely made it through a month of her newfound driving freedom when the oil light popped up on the dashboard while driving home from school. Falsely assuming that she had plenty of oil to make it home, she kept driving.

When she finally pulled into her parents' driveway, the poor car was smoking and clattering terribly. The engine was completely burnt up and beyond repair. The warning light had been there, but she wasn't quite mature enough to heed it.

Paul had some warning lights for the church in Colossae:

We tell others about Christ, warning everyone and teaching everyone with all the wisdom God has given us. We want to present them to God, perfect in their relationship to Christ (Colossians 1:28 NLT).

The verb *to warn* is "to advise on the consequences of a wrong action." Paul knew that if we are immature in Christ, then our likelihood of making wrong decisions is far greater than if we are actively walking in wisdom and light.

Yet the more that we read God's Word, sit under sound pastoral care, and surround ourselves with godly friendships, the more likely we are to heed the warning lights and make more right decisions than wrong.

Warning lights are there for our protection. They are an indicator that we should immediately pull over and get the help we need from the One who can provide it. If we are mature enough to heed the warning light, then we'll be back up and running in no time.

FATHER, LET US HAVE THE MATURITY TO TAKE
YOUR WARNING LIGHTS SERIOUSLY. THANK YOU
FOR YOUR PROTECTION, AND GIVE US WISDOM TO
MAKE MORE RIGHT DECISIONS THAN WRONG.

COMFORTING OTHERS

Have you ever been through a time of terrible pain or suffering and wondered what the purpose of it was? Perhaps it was excruciating physical pain or a messy divorce or even the unthinkable loss of a child.

Truly this is one of the hardest things to reconcile within our lives as a Christian. Why would a God who is good and all-powerful allow such heartache to wrench our souls? The answer is that we simply don't know. All we can know for certain is that if we have resolved to put our hope in the Lord and trust Him, then He promises to comfort us through our suffering.

More importantly, we can find purpose in the pain when we use it as an opportunity to comfort others.

The apostle Paul went through serious periods of suffering in his life, but he resolved to use them as a way to encourage others, saying,

He always comes alongside us to comfort us in every suffering so that we can come alongside those who are in any painful trial. We can bring them this same comfort that God has poured out upon us (II Corinthians 1:4 TPT).

What is it that you have suffered? If it's infertility, perhaps you could minister to other couples who are experiencing the same hardship. Or maybe you could be a friend to someone who has special needs. Have you broken free from addiction? Turning your suffering into a way to point others to the Healer is such a brave and admirable thing to do.

It's there that we find the purpose for our pain and can encourage others to keep the faith. God is still good and He pours out His love and comfort to all who seek Him.

> GOD, WE TRUST YOU EVEN WHEN LIFE
> IS HARD. THANK YOU FOR COMFORTING
> US IN EVERY SUFFERING, AND LET US BE
> WILLING TO DO THE SAME FOR OTHERS.

WORTHY BECAUSE OF HIM

On a scale of one to ten, how worthy do you feel at the moment? How deserving are you of love, attention, responsibility, or respect? Do you deem yourself to be "good enough" or "not good enough" and why?

Worthiness is a concept that all of us struggle with from time to time, even if we are walking in the light. We desperately want to be found worthy, but insecurities come calling and knock us off course.

Moses shared in the struggle to be found worthy even as God was speaking directly to him from a burning bush. When God told him to go to Egypt so that he could lead God's children out of slavery, Moses's response was, "Who am I?" Moses let his insecurity dictate his worthiness to get the job done.

But God reminds Moses that it's not who Moses is but who HE IS that makes Moses worthy of such a task. Exodus 3:14 ESV tell us

that God said to Moses, "I AM WHO I AM."

So you don't have be "good enough" or even try to figure it all out. Just go and He'll take care of the rest.

Have you and God ever had a similar conversation? "Who am I, Lord, to lead a small group?" "Who am I to sing on the worship team?" "Who am I to go on that mission trip?" And He says to you, "The question isn't who you are; the answer is who I AM!"

When we stop trying to make ourselves worthy, then we find that we actually are worthy because of who God is! He places His light inside of us and equips us for the job that He is calling us to do. We don't have to be "good enough" when He is better than enough! We are deserving of a higher calling not on our own merit, but because He alone is worthy.

GOD, WE SHAKE OFF OUR INSECURITIES JUST LIKE
MOSES DID, AND WE FIND OUR WORTHINESS IN YOU.

BE A THERMOSTAT

One bright Sunday a group of eighty-nine women returned home from an intense and beautiful spiritual retreat. They were keenly aware that their time together was rapidly coming to an end, but the rich worship continued in each of their hearts like a fire!

As they entered the sanctuary, their excitement over all they had seen the Lord do over the weekend was evident. They boldly approached the throne of grace with hands raised high in gratitude and worship.

As the pastor took the stage, he made this statement, "A thermometer is useful for reading the current temperature, but a thermostat SETS the temperature. Today these ladies are the thermostat that has lit this place on fire!"

What a great analogy! We have the same opportunity to be not just a thermometer in our spiritual lives but the thermostat, setting the temperature of our lives and the lives of those who are around us.

Paul told Timothy that he was to be bold with the gifts that the Lord had given him. In fact, in II Timothy 1:6–7 (The Message), he said,

The special gift of ministry you received when I laid hands on you and prayed—keep that ablaze! God doesn't want us to be shy with His gifts, but bold and loving and sensible.

He wanted Timothy to be ablaze with passion as he served the Lord because he knew that others would follow Timothy's lead.

When others look at our walk with the Lord, do they see a person who is only slightly illuminated, letting her light shine only when she's around other Christians? Or do they see a woman who is totally lit up for the Lord and is radiating His heat and light to everyone that she comes into contact with?

Are we content to read the temperature, allowing someone else to dictate if we are hot or cold? Or are we actively setting the temperature around us, dialing up the heat day by day?

He has set us ablaze not only for our own benefit but so that we can boldly shine for Him.

LORD, LET US BE A THERMOSTAT ON FIRE FOR YOU!

YOUR BRIGHT FUTURE

Grace has called your name. You once were stained, but now you are clean. When you thought that there was no hope, God set your feet on solid ground and redirected your steps. No longer do you sit in darkness, but rather you have been called into His marvelous light.

You are a new creation, His special treasure. You are chosen for greatness. He has big plans for you and they are going to far exceed anything that you could ever ask Him for or imagine. He will give you the vision to see if you look toward the light and trust Him. You do this by abiding in Him, meaning that you intentionally spend time reading His Word. You are daily seeking His wisdom for your life. You are having regular conversations with the One who knows you better than anyone else. In I Peter 2:9–10 (HCSB), it says,

> But you are a chosen race, a royal priesthood,
> a holy nation, a people for His possession,
> so that you may proclaim the praises
> of the One who called you out of darkness
> into His marvelous light.
> Once you were not a people,
> but now you are God's people;
> you had not received mercy,
> but now you have received mercy.

Because you have such an intimate relationship with your Father, you now have access to all the blessings and favor that belong to those of royal birth. However, being given such authority means that you must use it wisely. The purpose of this gracious gift is so that you will point others to the light. Reach your hands to heaven and proclaim the praises of the One who saved your life.

You will never be ashamed of what Jesus has done for you and refuse to hide your light under a basket. The world may not understand your light, but remember that light is attractive. Jesus is attractive. Your job is not to produce the light, it is simply to shine His light. You just be you, and He will do the rest.

Once you were nothing, but now you are God's highly favored and blessed daughter. You have received mercy. You have been made to shine. Your future is unbelievably bright.

O LORD, WHAT CAN WE SAY BUT THANK YOU!
MAY YOU BE GLORIFIED EACH AND EVERY DAY
AS WE SHINE BRIGHTLY FOR YOU ALONE!

If you have never responded to the Light of Christ, today is the day to have His Light fill you. The author, April Rodgers, would welcome the opportunity to pray with you. You can contact her at april_rodgers@icloud.com.

LIVE YOUR FAITH

Dear Friend,

     This book was prayerfully crafted with you, the reader, in mind—every word, every sentence, every page—was thoughtfully written, designed, and packaged to encourage you...right where you are this very moment. At DaySpring, our vision is to see every person experience the life-changing message of God's love. So, as we worked through rough drafts, design changes, edits and details, we prayed for you to deeply experience His unfailing love, indescribable peace, and pure joy. It is our sincere hope that through these Truth-filled pages your heart will be blessed, knowing that God cares about you—your desires and disappointments, your challenges and dreams.

He knows. He cares. He loves you unconditionally.

BLESSINGS!
THE DAYSPRING BOOK TEAM

**Additional copies of this book and
other DaySpring titles can be purchased
at fine retailers everywhere.
Order online at dayspring.com
or
by phone at 1-877-751-4347**